Clap Hands for the
Singing Molecatcher

Clap Hands for the Singing Molecatcher

Scenes from a Scottish Childhood

Roderick Grant

with line drawings by Robert Field

ORIGIN

This edition published in 2019 by
Origin, an imprint of Birlinn Ltd
West Newington House
10 Newington Road
Edinburgh
EH9 1QS

www.birlinn.co.uk

First published in 2007 by Birlinn Ltd

ISBN 978 1 912476 68 8

British Library Cataloguing-in-Publication Data
A catalogue record for this book is available
from the British Library

Typesetting and origination by Brinnoven, Livingston
Printed and bound by Clays Ltd, Elcograf S.p.A.

Author's Note

As a small boy I was constantly being reminded that I should be seen and not heard. I followed this advice as best I could – and when the mood took me. Until now. Because of this some names have been changed in order that no-one need feel too embarrassed by my delving into the memories of my childhood days.

Fair the day shine as it shone on my childhood –
Fair shine the day on the house with open door;
Birds come and cry there and twitter in the chimney –
But I go for ever and come again no more.

Robert Louis Stevenson

1

On my first day at school I walked two miles to get there, yelling and screaming all the while, accompanied by my mother, a large and mischievous jackdaw, a breathless terrier who barked continuously and a large brown paper bag containing thickly cut sandwiches of home-made raspberry jam.

As we trudged across the fields I cried and sobbed. The tears blinded me so that I had to be dragged along, stumbling and shuffling. I clutched the bag against my chest with one hand, while the other was held tightly by my mother. 'Just in case you try to run off, my lad,' is what she said.

Overhead, my pet jackdaw wheeled and dived, cawing and croaking his delight at this new adventure in the fresh, early morning sun; and our little cairn terrier ran barking through the long, seeding grass, burrowing and bobbing among the waving stalks as she struggled to keep pace. Walking, running or flying our various modes of travel took us over several fields, in one of which a herd of cattle stampeded at first sight of this strange and noisy procession, through a wood smelling of ferns and moss and long-decayed leaves and along the gorse-bedecked banks of a tumbling stream. And there, between the main road and the railway line, with a dark forest of tall, swaying pine trees in the background, was the schoolhouse and school. To me on that tear-stained morning it might as well have been the county gaol.

Two hours later, when no-one was looking, the moment was

right. I escaped. I ran away, down the path, across the road, over the fields, through the wood, as fast as my legs could carry me. The jam sandwiches had been eaten. I was hungry. And home was the only place where more food could be found. As I fled my place of captivity home meant two things to me: food – and freedom once again.

My jackdaw, perched atop the woodshed, rose chattering into the air, dive-bombing my diminutive figure before I had even reached the fence between field and garden. The terrier, sitting on the stile gazing wistfully into space, greeted my return with a bout of enthusiastic barking; the jackdaw, screeching and squawking, dropped with flailing wings and perched on my shoulder. And my mother, drawn from the kitchen by this sudden outburst of noise, was not amused.

I was given no time to explain; no time to get indoors to assuage my gnawing hunger. Leaving her apron hanging on the fence I was taken, sometimes by the ear, sometimes by the elbow, and propelled back across the fields and through the wood to where the schoolmistress awaited to add a few strong words to those of my mother's still ringing inside my head. But her scolding came with a mug of hot, sweet cocoa which she poured herself while delivering the lecture. My mother stood embarrassed beside me, nodding her head in agreement with the terms of this, my first official, formal warning, while outside the terrier barked in the playground and the jackdaw sat on a window ledge and attacked the glass. Once more I was incarcerated against my will and my mother returned home, accompanied by dog and jackdaw, to a house filled with smoke and the smell of blackened, burning scones.

While indoors attending to the baking disaster, the terrier now left to her own devices decided to make the trip once again and set off for the fifth time to cover the two-mile journey. My drooping spirits were revived when, during the singing of a hymn, I heard once again the familiar bark as she dashed around the playground leaping up now and then beneath the high windows. An older pupil was sent to investigate and returned moments later clutching the struggling dog who was fervently licking his face. I rose from my desk, shedding a tear and dog and boy were reunited amid scenes of joy, grief and general mirth from the other occupants of the classroom.

Shortly afterwards my mother arrived in hot pursuit, red of face, breathless, and full of apologies for the fuss being caused that day by her offspring and assorted pets. The schoolmistress helpfully suggested that I be taken home early – there not being much left of the school day by this time – adding that perhaps, by tomorrow, I might be in a more settled frame of mind. My mother, a trifle too eagerly I felt, assured her that she would see to it that indeed I would be more settled. 'And better behaved,' she added ominously. The schoolmistress nodded her approval. Slowly. There was a faint trace of a smile at the corners of her mouth.

So, back across the fields we trudged: boy, mother and dog. The jackdaw met us high above the trees and escorted us on the final homeward stretch. Once there, everyone was in a state of total exhaustion. My mother made herself a pot of tea. I was given a glass of milk. She sank into an armchair and I went into the garden to lie on the grass. The terrier lapped an entire bowl of water, then went to sleep among the hollyhocks in a corner of the herbaceous border. Only the jackdaw seemed capable of raising a spark of energy. This he used by perching on the wire roof of the hen run in order to preen his feathers, a deliberate ploy to annoy the four bantam cockerels who regarded this area as their sole territory. Very soon voices were raised and feathers were flying as the usual battle got underway. Normally, the commotion would have brought my mother running from the house to beat at the troublemakers with a handy stick. On that particular day she stayed indoors sipping her tea and the battle raged unchecked, hostilities only ceasing when the jackdaw soared up and into the sky to leave four angry bantams clucking among themselves about their bruises and loss of dignity.

It was 1946 and in the Scottish Highlands the summer sun beat down relentlessly day after day. Its probing heat baked all that it touched, turning the grass a dusty brown, making the branches of sapling trees wilt and droop where once they had hung fresh and proud. And in the maze of odd-shaped fields, bounded by dry-stone walls, the oats and barley ripened quickly until the landscape was a patchwork of dowdy green and rich, lustrous gold.

In the field at one side of the house I spent hours hunting the elusive disembodied 'cronking' of a pair of corncrakes, desperate not only for a sight of the birds, but for a glimpse of the nest and eggs. Everyone who heard the birds assured me there would be a nest, somewhere amid the forest of golden corn stalks. But I never found it. Neither did I ever see the birds. I listened to their monotonous calling through the twilight hours of the short, hot summer nights, my mind filled with their picture imprinted from a painting in my well-thumbed book of *British Birds, Their Nests and Eggs.* I imagined what a thrill it would be to actually see my very own corncrakes – even one of them – and I dreamed of actually fulfilling this ambition. But when I awoke each morning from my restless sleep the sound of the birds was the only tangible thing I had to possess. The corncrakes eventually departed as secretly and silently as they had first arrived; an anonymous pair who retained their privacy despite the determination to invade it shown by a five-year-old boy who lived for several months within earshot of their everyday lives.

I was an only child, living in an isolated and remote part of Scotland. Home was deep in the heart of a sprawling country estate where my father was gamekeeper to the man who owned thousands of acres of moor, forest and field – the laird. My mother kept house in addition to accomplishing a thousand

and one other daily tasks, ranging from chopping wood for the ever ravenous fire to milking the goats, feeding the ferrets and collecting the eggs from a noisy horde of squabbling, rebellious hens.

While growing to the age of five I had no human companion close at hand with whom to share the daily joy of play. The nearest house to my own was the mansion house – the Big House as it was referred to, sometimes in hushed, almost reverent tones, by the faithful living and working on the estate. This was about one mile away. In the other direction, also about a mile distant, was the church and manse, where the minister lived, and an imposing lodge, with gigantic gates, dominating the entrance to the main driveway which led to the Big House. This drive, tarred and immaculately maintained, ran through the estate for almost three miles, passing the front door of our house.

When it reached the Big House one branch forked towards the castellated portico of the main door, while the other veered to the right. This fork ran through the old stable yard, past the gardeners' cottages and alongside the vegetable gardens, to rejoin its earlier link some distance beyond the hallowed environs of the Big House. The distinction was clear-cut. No notice was required to warn the unwary traveller. Everyone knew instinctively that the way to the left – the route past the sprawling architecture of the Big House with its vast, green lawns and terraced gardens and uninterrupted view of a tumbling, rock-strewn river – was taboo to lesser mortals. Their road was to the right and even when the laird and his family were absent, as they were for the greater part of the year, in either Edinburgh or London, this demarcation was continued.

I expect the laird, his wife, children and guests merely wanted to retain their privacy, but as a small boy with a nose for troublesome questions I found the system both puzzling and faintly daft. When I was old enough to ride a bicycle and the estate's network of roads became my very own highways and byways I used to halt at the junction and consider the challenge. Then, as often as not, I would cycle boldly past the windows – row upon row of them – and front door of the Big House. Sometimes, as the gravel scrunched beneath the wheels, my nerve would fail and I would speed away, ears tensed for the first hint of trouble behind my back. But no Rolls-Royce ever pursued me, no threatening words were ever flung in my direction. There was once, all the same, when the son of one of the gardeners saw me defying the unwritten code and thought it prudent to tell my father. My father cuffed me around the ears and later, when the time was right, I got my revenge by thumping the gardener's son. Afterwards we became the best of friends and together, on creaking bicycles, raced each other along the forbidden highway.

The Second World War was already well underway when I was born amid the frosty gloom and intense cold of a January night in 1941. It had been snowing, on and off, for several days. At a quarter to midnight I arrived. So, too, did a howling gale and one of the fiercest blizzards of that winter.

My father was in the Seaforth Highlanders. My mother and I spent the war years in our home on the estate while in the fields and the woods beyond the garden the rabbits multiplied, running free in wild abandonment, cocking a snook at the farmers who bemoaned their burgeoning numbers. While men killed men and the world was in bloody turmoil they, at least, were safe from concentrated hostilities, there being no gamekeeper to keep them in check. It was a truce which was to end in a deadly day of reckoning when the war was over and my father returned, exchanging the grenades and .303 rifle for a twelve-bore shotgun and a pair of pink-eyed, bloodthirsty ferrets. But all that was in the future and for the years that remained they enjoyed their freedom, moving across the fields in the warm dusk like some vast army of silent, rampaging will-o'-the-wisps.

During the war the estate was used as a battle training school by the army. By day and by night the woods and surrounding moorland became simulated battlegrounds, hastily improvised rehearsals of secret campaigns yet to be launched in Norway, North Africa, Sicily, France and the forests of Burma. Paratroops in camouflaged helmets and uniforms seemed to be everywhere and, from the depths of my pram, I heard a strange and bewildering variety of unfamiliar accents – Canadian, American, Australian, French, cockney and Polish.

My mother supplied eggs to the officers billeted in the splendid spaciousness of the Big House and in return we feasted on illicit chocolate, tinned ham and a host of other delights far beyond the range of her ration book coupons and purse. Now and then the wife of one of the officers would stay with us while visiting her husband before he set off on a mission across the sea, but for most of the time we were alone.

It was a time of intense activity all around us, of noise and confusion. I lay in my cot and the sound of battle filled my head. While slow-moving bombers droned through darkened skies in and out of the RAF base on the Moray Firth coast at Kinloss, the windows rattled as machine guns barked and grenades thumped among the trees close to the house. These battles, waged with a deadly intensity, usually took place half a mile or more away from us. But one evening our war came even closer.

My mother sat beside the fire knitting socks. A few feet away I clung to the bars of my cot watching the flickering flames dancing around the logs in the grate, hearing the rapid clicking of the needles. On the table in the centre of the room a Tilley lamp hissed while the yellow mantle cast its soft light across my mother's face twisted in concentration at the task in hand. Shadows lurked in the far corners of the room and cast twisted shapes on the walls. But these held no terrors for me. They were a familiar, even welcoming sight, as was the sound of the big radio, powered by heavy accumulator batteries, bringing to us with green-lit dial and glowing valves the comfort of faraway voices, music and laughter. To me that huge radio, called the wireless by my mother, was a powerful, magical force full of mystery when it hummed and crackled, buzzed and whistled, prior to releasing a voice or a snatch of dance band music into the room.

There was a sudden burst of rifle fire, the whine of ricochets from guttering and chimney pots; the closer and much more terrifying noise of glass breaking. Something passed through the room, behind my mother's head and over the top of my cot. A pane of glass shattered in the window on the far side of the room. The firing continued. There was the distant sound of shouted commands and men's voices raised in reply. My mother dragged me from the cot and together we huddled against the wall alongside the chimney breast.

Ten minutes or so passed and the rifle shots grew more sporadic, then after several isolated cracks ceased entirely. Cautiously, my mother rose from the floor and went over to the window nearest to the fireplace. The black-out blind had a ragged tear in the bottom right-hand corner while behind it a neat, round hole had been punched through the glass. At the other window blind and curtains flapped in the draught. The window pane had vanished, except for a few jagged slivers of glass around the edges of the frame. My mother swore very rarely. The words she used that night I had never heard before. Nor do I think she ever used them again.

At first light she was out of the house and on her way to the Big House, my pram bumping and bouncing, reflecting both her energy and the anger seething within her. The commanding officer was routed from his bed and a complaint was made. Poor sleep-starved, weary soldier: he didn't stand a chance against my mother's wrath. He refused to believe that a bullet from any of the guns of the men under his command could have endangered civilian lives, let alone gone whining through our house.

'Then come and see for yourself,' was my mother's reply.

A jeep was summoned. The pram was hoisted aboard, held firm by a young soldier. My mother sat in front, holding me in her arms, beside the driver. The commanding officer sat in the back alongside the pram. At the house the worthy officer expressed amazement at the damage, strode off to look at the wood on the high bank behind the house. He returned several minutes later. He was both shame-faced and deeply apologetic. A row of dummy targets, shapeless bundles swathed in canvas sacking, had been scattered among the trees. Our house was just over the horizon in direct line of fire. They would be removed immediately, he said. Such a thing would never occur again.

'I would think not,' replied my mother, still grim-faced but now mellowing slightly having triumphed over the military mind.

When he left to return to his headquarters in the Big House the commanding officer clutched a paper bag containing several newly laid eggs, still warm from the straw where the hens had dropped them. The soldier and the driver shared a pot of blackcurrant jam. There were smiling faces on either side. From then on the chocolate, corned beef, tinned ham and fruit from the officers' kitchen at the Big House seemed to arrive with greater frequency and in larger quantities. The targets vanished and we were safe from death and destruction.

The pane of glass was replaced (at the army's expense) but the hole in the other window was left, plugged in winter by a wad of cardboard, the source of discussion for years to come after arms were laid down and men across the world returned to their homeland once again to live in peace.

2

When I was three I was stung 172 times by a swarm of angry, demented bees. And as my mother said later when my head, face and neck had returned to a reasonably normal shape, 'It was all your own fault.'

Of course it was. But for a three-year-old boy roaming among the fruit bushes, heavy with bloated, juice-filled currants, shining red and glossy black, what better fun was there after having gorged himself on the plump, ripe berries than to lunge with a pointed stick at the narrow opening to the two white-painted hives?

First one, then the other, back and fore between the two, rattling and prodding the mysterious interiors, cackling delightedly at the first hints of the terrible revenge about to be exacted. Initially, a few bees took to the air to dive-bomb my darting figure. I ignored their buzzing protests and concentrated my efforts on stirring with frenetic glee the interior of the hive built like a miniature house, complete with wooden chimney pots and wood-tiled roof. The inhabitants decided to repel the irritating invader by using sheer force of numbers.

They poured through the slit and sought out the source of their anger. In a long, thin black line they rose into the air above my head, then dropped straight on to it. I had no time to run more than a few paces before the first of the stings was delivered. My ears were choked by the high-pitched humming made by their flailing wings. They quickly became a swarm as in their dozens they landed on me, crawling into my hair, beneath my shirt, the noise growing louder, the strength of their attack more ferocious.

I tripped and fell, sprawling on the grass of the drying-green. I tried to rise as the loathsome crowd descended and for several seconds saw momentary glimpses of blue sky and trees, of clouds, the roof of the house, before the enlarged swarm was totally upon me and my eyes became gummed, as were my ears, by this determined army of maddened avengers.

The bees fell on my body as if they wished to devour me. The pain from the stings and the dreadful noise of the concentrated attack made me scream and go on screaming until my lungs choked through lack of air. Several bees entered my open mouth. I felt their barbed stings pierce the tender skin around my lips. I screamed even louder than before, struggling to rise once again from beneath the black, twisting, turning swarm. I got to my knees, clawing at my head and neck, then collapsed unconscious.

My mother, entering the kitchen to fill the kettle in order to make a pot of tea for herself and a visiting friend, glanced out of the window and saw the swirling mass of bees. She called to the friend to join her in watching the swarm, rising and falling in the air between the hives and the rows of fruit bushes. The kettle dropped into the sink from her trembling fingers when through a gap in the black, shapeless cloud she saw my prostrate figure. Together, they rushed into the garden, plunging without a thought for their own safety into the humming throng.

I was grabbed by the arms and pulled across the grass. The bees followed. Then half lifting, half carrying me the two women rushed me through the garden and into the kitchen. The door was slammed on the pursuing swarm and the windows tightly fastened. My face, neck and shoulders were covered in stings, as were my legs and hands. Dying bees crawled their last journey upon my body and I lay on the kitchen floor as their living, angry companions beat against the glass, still possessed by the deep fury which my stupidity had unleashed.

My mother's friend was sent to the Big House to ask for help from one of the army doctors. She left the house by the front door, far away from the marauding bees, and ran across the garden to one of the sheds where her bicycle was propped against the wall. While she cycled in search of help my mother started to remove the stings from my skin where their barbs held them fast after having broken away from the bodies of the bees. One by one she killed the maimed and dying bees. She applied a solution of baking soda and water to my fever-hot skin.

When I regained consciousness she had me in her arms as she knelt on the floor. Beside her was a mound of small black carcasses where she had dropped the bees she found. In the garden, beyond the window, the bees had returned to their hives, well satisfied by the spirited defence of their territory. All was quiet once again. My head throbbed with an intense pain. My neck and shoulders were on fire. I saw my mother shaking her head in a gesture of resignation at my foolishness, she having warned me on several occasions to stay away from the vicinity of the hives.

The doctor arrived, drugs were administered and I was put to bed. I stayed there for several days, eating little but drinking a lot in order to quench an overpowering thirst. When I had fully recovered and the time had come once again for me to venture forth into the garden stern warnings were issued by my mother about what would happen to me if ever again I dared to go near the two beehives. Even worse would be my fate, she assured me, if I should be foolish enough to repeat my experiment of annoying the bees by rattling a stick inside the hives. (Bit by bit I had confessed to what had precipitated the attacks, while lying in bed recovering from my ordeal).

I promised to obey on both counts. They were easy promises

to keep. For quite some time I would run like a scalded cat if a bee came within twenty feet of me. All the same, now and then, when life was particularly boring and in need of the injection of some excitement, I would crawl beneath the branches of the currant bushes, there to sit and gaze at the bees entering and leaving their hives a safe distance away. The fearful knowledge of what they had done to me and would no doubt do again if I went closer kept me at bay, rooted to the spot by an eerie, spine-tingling vision of horror.

The army doctor who treated me was to die several months later during a mock battle in the grounds of the estate. Four others died that day: three soldiers and a nurse. Several people were wounded. The search by the military authorities for absolute realism in training their troops had, not for the first time, taken yet another macabre twist.

Live ammunition and primed grenades were being used. Nothing was simulated. If one of the 'enemy' showed himself as a target he was liable to be fired upon. The idea was to shoot very close to, but just over, the head of the 'enemy'. However, such was the enthusiasm of the defenders of a small wood flanking a wide, deep pond that when the opposing forces appeared over the brow of the opposite hill, leading steeply down to the water's edge, a hail of bullets was unleashed against them.

Two soldiers died on their way down the slope. And when the men started to swim across the weed-clogged surface of the pond a burst of machine-gun fire killed one of those in the water and badly wounded three others. The wild tracery of bullets found their way through a dense thicket of rhododendron bushes, beside the stream at the head of the pond, and went into a waiting ambulance. The doctor and one of two nurses were killed. The other nurse and the driver of the ambulance were wounded.

The doctor's wife came north from Glasgow and stayed with my mother for several days while the formalities of sudden death were dispensed with. Before she married, my mother had been a nurse in a Glasgow hospital and had known the doctor then. I listened to the sound of the woman's grief and heard the soothing words intoned by my mother and was bewildered by the effects of the tragedy. Happiness and laughter were what I thrived on best of all and during the time the sorrowing woman stayed in our house a dark mood of depression encircled me. Not even the pleasures and mysteries contained in the sunlit summer woods were powerful enough to lift it from my saddened heart and sagging spirits.

3

A few months after my fourth birthday a small, black bundle
of feathers was handed to me by my father, at home for
a spell of leave. The bundle stirred beneath my fingers and
a head and neck emerged. Two bead-like eyes, shining as if
polished, regarded me warily. The head moved swiftly, stabbing
the long beak into a finger. I cried out and dropped the bird.
It landed on the gravel path in an undignified heap, but made
no attempt to escape, being too young to fly. Instead it looked
up at us and squawked loudly, balancing its ungainly body on
two spindly legs.

This was my introduction to the jackdaw, the first pet I ever
had. Others to follow were rabbits, a tortoise, dogs, a young
fox, a woodpigeon, a goat, a chicken, goldfish, bullfinches,
a canary, budgerigars, and perhaps most exotic of all, two
young hen harriers. The jackdaw, however, became my constant
companion in all manner of mischievous enterprises.

He had been found in the garden of an estate worker and given
to my father because jackdaws figured in the estate's proscribed
list of birds and animals liable to summary execution if found
within breathing distance of the prized and much coveted game
birds, pheasant, partridge and red grouse. For the birds this
list was headed by that arch-villain the hooded crow, mean and
cunning in its relentless efforts to rob other birds of either eggs
or young chicks. It went on through the falcons and hawks, but
omitted the kestrel which was reprieved because no case had
ever been (or ever would be) proved against it. Owls, magpies

and jays also featured prominently. Animal offenders had stoats, weasels, rats and foxes as the main prey.

Jackdaws were rather a peripheral case, viewed by my father, at least, as more like a gang of unruly hooligans than dedicated, determined killers. Having a habit of flying around in small, noisy groups they were more irritating than dangerous. Their nuisance value reached its greatest height when they descended on the hens' and chickens' feeding ground to go strutting about helping themselves to tasty morsels. They would also lunge in bullying fashion at the tiny chicks who got in the way, sending them fleeing into the bushes. There they would remain for hours, cheeping in terror, until rounded up by my mother and returned to the by now almost demented broody hens. As this always happened during the early evening feed it often meant my mother having to crawl around with a torch or a sputtering hurricane lamp, searching the undergrowth as the first of the owls hooted in the darkened woods and the foxes barked their message that now was the time when they were abroad.

Despite the marauding jackdaws and the almost nightly nocturnal search parties organised by my mother, who, quite naturally, vowed wrath on the heads of the impudent birds causing her so much trouble, my father never lifted a shotgun in their direction. I think he had a soft spot for their saucy behaviour, their air of total nonchalance and, when in a gang, their rowdy, boisterous, show-off mannerisms. So, the baby jackdaw was given to me. I called him Jack.

He was fed on bread and milk, augmented by a mixture of small beetles, woodlice and worms caught for him by me on determined and diligent forays around the garden. It did not take him long to realise that when I turned over a stone there was likely to be something tasty (although repulsive to me) slithering about in the full glare of daylight. In he would dart and help himself, croaking loudly the extent of his pleasure when the morsel was swallowed, cocking his head to one side as he awaited further treasures beneath yet more stones.

Within a few days he was balancing precariously on my shoulders like Long John Silver's parrot in *Treasure Island*. Unfortunately, he was infested by horrible, black fleas, many of which made a swift exit to seek a change of diet among my hair. My mother, already wary of this new close friend I had acquired, now had the golden opportunity to point out to both myself and my father the problems likely to arise if Jack was allowed to stay. The fleas were just the first of what, she warned, would be an endless catalogue of trouble.

There then followed a period of intense bargaining when various concessions were, somewhat grudgingly, made by either side. But the outcome was in my favour. And Jack's. He was allowed to stay. My mother was adamant on one point, however: he was never again to be allowed to enter the house. He could live in the woodshed. The cardboard box in which he had spent the first few nights with us was hastily removed from the kitchen and just as quickly I was plunged into the bath. There I was scrubbed and my head vigorously shampooed free of the offending mites. All the time this was happening I could hear Jack squawking in the garden while inside the steam-filled room my mother muttered strange incantations against him as she rubbed at my hair and the soap ran freely into my eyes.

Barring Jack from entering the house was not a simple task. It is quite surprising the number of times in any given day that a young boy decides to go indoors, sometimes for no more than a few minutes. In order to do this I had quickly to adopt a great deal of subterfuge so that Jack was left behind. At first it was easy. Not being able to fly I could leave him on the grass and run towards the kitchen door, while behind me an agitated and squawking bird hopped and slithered across the ground. Easiest of all, when I thought about it, was simply to lock him in the woodshed in the box which served as home.

But as soon as he learned to fly he was his own master, matching any cunning I had with much more initiative of his own. He could not then be locked in the shed because the structure was decidedly rickety and he could escape quite easily. There were plenty of holes in the wooden walls. He quickly developed the ability to sense when I was about to part company with him to go indoors. Or, quite simply, he just used his busy brain to work things out for himself; such as when we would be playing happily around the garden or in the field and my mother would come to the door and shout that a meal was ready, adding the usual instruction that I was to 'Hurry up'.

Off Jack would go, out of reach into the sky, swooping and diving, circling the house. Then, as I drew close to the door he would fly straight towards it if it was open. It was then up to either my mother or myself to bar entry to the fast-flying bird. If I felt I would never reach the kitchen in time I would shout a warning. Instantaneously my mother would appear flapping a tea towel or brandishing a ladle. Up Jack would soar, chattering angrily, to perch on the guttering or the slate-covered roof. I raced inside. The door was slammed against him.

Jack's banishment from the house also meant that the windows could only be left open by a mere fraction. So adept was he at wriggling through the smallest gap it was best to leave them tightly shut. So, there in the kitchen, on the hottest summer day we would sit sweating, eating our meal while Jack paraded up and down on the window ledge banging on the glass with his long, sharp beak.

Of course to me all this was the greatest fun. To my mother it must have been both frustrating and irritating to have to run the gauntlet each time she entered or left the house. Even going to the washing line became a drama with me being sent on ahead to scout for signs of the elusive bird. In time he grew more crafty and took to perching quietly on the guttering directly above the kitchen door. He would wait until the door was open then drop down like some dark spectre from the sky to try, usually unsuccessfully, to gain entry. On more than one occasion my mother, startled out of her wits by this black shadow descending almost on to her head, dropped freshly washed clothes or hot ashes from the fire as she shrieked in alarm and beat out with both hands at the creature who refused to play the game and obey the clear-cut rules.

It had to happen sooner or later. It was obvious. The law of averages was in Jack's favour. I went indoors one day and left the kitchen door wide open. My mother was doing housework in the bedrooms. A large bowl of steaming custard, which she had just made, stood on the kitchen table. It was a Sunday and visitors were expected in the afternoon. Everything in the house was dust free, polished, swept, sparkling. All was shipshape in Bristol fashion, ready for inspection.

While I ran to the kitchen sink to pour a glass of water Jack sailed through the open doorway in total silence hardly able, I expect, to believe his good fortune. He landed, with wildly beating wings, dead centre in the bowl of custard. As the hot, sticky liquid enveloped his feet, legs and belly feathers he squawked with a loud and despairing cry. For several seconds he struggled wildly, spraying custard across the room, then rose slowly like some creature escaping from a quicksand, flapping his wings, pulling himself clear of the bowl.

It was then that my mother entered the room. Her shriek matched Jack's horrified squawking. Rushing at him she tried to strike him in mid-air with a duster. I stood transfixed beside the sink as my mother lunged this way and that around the room before scoring a direct hit. Jack sank swiftly towards the floor, but recovered sufficiently to land once again on the table. My mother dived, hands outstretched to grasp hold of him. The jackdaw twisted away out of reach and was in the air again, sending blobs of custard flying everywhere.

There were two brackets on the walls, each holding a paraffin lamp. Thinking he would be safe there Jack flew up to one of them and tried to perch. With sticky feet he found it extremely difficult to get a grip. Clawing and scrabbling and flapping his wings he covered the lamp with custard before dislodging the glass chimney and sending it crashing on to the floor. The noise and sight of the breaking glass goaded my mother into greater fury. She beat at his feet with the flailing duster, trying to dislodge him from his precarious perch. Custard was now running freely down the wall.

Jack took off again, chattering loudly, hopped along the length of the window sill, smearing the surface with custard and knocking over several ornaments together with a much-coveted geranium in an earthenware pot. He then jumped down and landed on a pile of newly ironed clothes, depositing more of the yellow, glutinous mess across shirts, blouses, pyjamas and underwear. Goaded now beyond endurance my mother made a determined onslaught and hurled the duster at him. Jack was hit broadside and swept on to the floor. Grabbing hold of a brush my mother rushed at him and in a single movement pushed him through the doorway and down the steps. Jack landed in a heap on the gravel path, caught sight of my mother still in pursuit and fled, complaining volubly, to the safety of some high trees at the edge of the field.

No such swift escape was possible for me. My mother surveyed the damage. A film of custard coated almost every surface in the room: walls, rugs, table and window sill. The level in the bowl had dropped alarmingly and the neatly ironed clothes had now become the next day's washing. Suffice to say I was physically punished and verbally mauled and sent flying from the kitchen with almost as much undignified haste as Jack had made his departure.

I refused to return for my meal and instead went into a long, deep sulk, skulking in the wood with a sticky and extremely chastened friend. Together, later in the day, we watched the visitors arriving, peering from the depths of the bushes as we listened to the conversation and heard questions asked about my health and general welfare. My mother explained that for the moment I was in disgrace and in great detail gave her account (extremely one-sided, I thought) of the nuisance I had been and how the jackdaw was 'a proper little pest and no mistake'. I stroked Jack's flea-infested feathers and reassured him he was no pest. He seemed to accept what I said and kept quiet except for what seemed like a low chuckle from deep down in his throat.

Having kept out of sight for several hours I decided to make a triumphal and spectacular reappearance. How the idea took shape in my head I was never to know. I merely emerged from my hiding place and did it. My father's spaniel prowled back and fore behind the bars of his kennel waiting for his evening meal. My mother and visitors were on the path in front of the house. They saw me come around the corner and talk to the dog. Yelping and barking it jumped up and down, licking my outstretched hand. I then pulled off my shirt and thrust it at the dog. He pulled one way, I pulled the other. It was a high-spirited game of 'tug-of-war'. The cloth split instantly. Off came my shorts. Within seconds they had suffered a similar fate. Next came vest and underpants. Now into the game completely, the spaniel tore and scratched, snarled and growled, reducing them to tattered shreds. Clutching the pieces between his teeth he rushed inside to deposit them in the straw on his bed. He returned, barking loudly, eager for more.

All I had left were my shoes and socks. I kept them on and with a series of whoops like a demented Red Indian brave I danced naked in front of the excited dog, then raced for the safety of the wood. Behind me there were shouts of astonishment, the sustained barking of the dog and somewhere in the sky high above it all Jack looked down and chattered freely his own reaction to events.

4

One of the first questions asked of a new pupil at the primary school was if he or she could sing any hymns. There were two other five-year-old boys starting school along with me. One was the son of a farmer from a remote farm out on the moor, the other a farm worker's son from a neighbouring property. Both had older sisters already attending the school so were less in awe of their surroundings than me.

The teacher beamed reassuringly at the three round, apprehensive faces staring up at her formidable figure after the various mothers had departed.

'What hymn are you familiar with?' she asked the farm worker's son.

He looked tongue-tied and crestfallen. He shuffled his boots on the wooden floor. Behind us the other pupils, boys and girls up to the age of twelve all sharing the one classroom, waited in expectation. There was a lengthy pause.

'You don't know one, I take it,' said the teacher eventually. She stood behind her high lectern-type desk, hands gripping the edges, and stared down at the uncomfortable boy.

'No, miss,' came the whispered reply. A look of shame crossed his features as if he had just been forced to confess to some particularly odious crime.

'Never mind,' was the teacher's answer. 'In a day or two I expect we will have changed this unhappy state of affairs.'

The boy blinked rapidly in wary incomprehension as she turned her attention to the farmer's son. The schoolmistress smiled warmly at him. She knew she was on safer ground here. His father was an elder of the church.

'And you, James,' she said, 'what hymn do you know best?'

James's face, flushed with an inner glow of superiority, beamed in triumph. His chest was out, his back was straight, as he answered proudly, '"*Jesus Loves Me*".'

The teacher's smile was warm and benevolent. It radiated approval, a fact quickly noted by James who smiled sweetly in return.

'Good,' she said. 'Very good indeed. In a few moments we will get you to sing it for us.'

Her gaze now focused on me. I was not to be outdone. I had no intention of being upstaged. Already, I could sense that James had ingratiated himself to a considerable degree due to his ready knowledge of religious music. My answer was out before the inevitable question was asked.

'I know the words of "The Muckin' o' Geordie's Byre",' I said.

At this the other pupils dissolved in laughter, the boys pushing and nudging each other, girls whispering among themselves, giggling; all glancing between my face and that of the schoolmistress whose rosy cheeks seemed a little rosier and whose lips were twitching in a determined effort to stifle a smile.

Little wonder. 'The Muckin' o' Geordie's Byre' told the story in a series of rousing verses of the attempts of a drunken and careless farm worker to clean his boss's cowshed.

'That is not what I mean by a hymn,' she said at last after hushing the pupils with a grim stare at the bobbing heads and shuffling figures. She turned to James.

'What is a hymn, James?'

'A song you sing in church, miss. In praise of the Lord.'

'Good boy. Good boy.'

She was looking at me again.

'Have you ever heard your cow byre song sung in church?'

I couldn't quite grasp what all the fuss was about. But of one thing I was certain. James had done it again. He was grinning from ear to ear. I was rapidly losing ground.

'Yes, miss,' I replied firmly. 'Often.'

At once the laughter erupted behind me, quickly stifled by a glare from the teacher and three rapid bangs on the lid of her desk.

'In that case,' she said, giving me a long, hard stare, 'you can sing it for us all if you wish.'

James looked decidedly miffed at this decision and stared at me warily. I was obviously the sort of heathen who undoubtedly in the years since his birth he had been warned about by his father, mother and even more religious grandmother. Who could blame him, really? The 'hymn' I had chosen was a rowdy and mildly bawdy bothy ballad, one of the many songs of farmyard life which unmarried workers gathered in their spartan accommodation sang on long winter nights when the day's work was done and there were hours to spare without toil. It had no religious content whatsoever, except for a brief and not entirely complimentary mention of a minister of the church. But by the age of five I had learnt by heart the words of several songs and this, above all, was my favourite.

After James had squeaked and slithered his excruciating way through 'Jesus Loves Me' I gave a spirited rendering of my choice, shouting with relish the oft-repeated chorus, all this accompanied on the piano with great spirit and a certain degree of flair and panache by a teacher whose head bobbed rhythmically in time to the thumping beat of the music. I enjoyed my first taste of singing to an audience. And my chest swelled with pride when the teacher said loudly as I went to my desk,

'You have a fine singing voice. We must make sure it is used to good purpose.'

Whether or not she meant it should not be squandered on tub-thumping renditions of bothy ballads, but on finer, purer music, I had, of course, no way of knowing. But as she spoke there was a distinct twinkle in her eye and later in the day, as she wrote some arithmetic problems on the large dust-covered blackboard, rocking on its chipped and battered easel, I heard once again the tune of my favourite song being whistled, quite softly, through her firmly clenched teeth.

The teacher, stout and unmarried, lived with her sister in the schoolhouse which formed part of the school building. To us pupils the house was 'tied on to the school'. When spoken of together when stalls were being arranged for sales of work or invitations issued for special functions in the community hall, they were always referred to as the Misses Milne. This form of address intrigued me. The teacher was called Isabella and her sister, as thin and spindly as her sister was stout and formidable, was called May. There was another sister called Rosebud who came to stay at various times of the year. I had never heard of anyone being called Rosebud and as I grew older and slightly more bold (or cheeky) I tried as often as possible by asking various questions to get Miss Milne to speak about her sister so that I could hear the magical name being repeated in her lovely, soft West Highland accent with its lilting and rolling cadences.

For a couple of years after I started school in 1946 there was no school meals service. Pupils brought sandwiches and wedges of cake which were eaten during the lunchtime break, if not consumed before then as mine were more often than not. These were washed down with a large brown enamel mug of hot, sweet cocoa, made in the schoolhouse by Miss May and transported by her from there to the classroom in one of the biggest enamel kettles I had ever seen. It, too, was brown and much chipped. Miss May also provided the cocoa for the mid-morning break, entering the classroom after a timid knock on the door and advancing on tiptoe, kettle aloft, to the large table against a wall where, routine dictated, the requisite number of brown mugs would be waiting. I became quite obsessed by the size of the kettle, watching it with incredulous eyes, as with one hand on the top handle and the other on the handle on the rear she expertly filled the mugs, nodding deferentially to her waiting sister, then withdrew, always backwards, still on tiptoe, as if leaving the presence of royalty.

I longed to be given the job of carrying the kettle which came up from time to time when Miss May had a cold and in order to save her the walk in the open air from schoolhouse to classroom one of the older boys would be sent to fetch it at the appropriate time. But I was too small and puny for such a task. I knew it and resented the fact. I consoled myself with the knowledge that one day when I was bigger it would, most certainly, be my turn to collect and carry the coveted kettle. However long I was prepared to wait.

Alas, the Government introduced free milk in the mornings and meals in the middle of the day. With one blow my ambitions and hopes were dashed to the ground. Overnight Miss May and her kettle became redundant.

It was to be several years before I was to see the kettle again. Along with several other boys I was digging and planting vegetables in the schoolhouse garden. Seed potatoes were going into the ground, holes were being prepared for cabbage plants and leeks. There, in a patch of nettles, in a corner of the sprawling, semi-wild garden, it lurked on its side, rusting and chipped, beneath the high, sweet-scented hawthorn hedge. A robin had made her nest in the depths of where once our cocoa had been brewed and four squawking heads thrust upwards, beaks agape, demanding to be fed.

When I first attended school there were twenty-five pupils crammed into the tiny classroom. Later, this was to dwindle to around fifteen, due mainly to the departure from the district of a large family of six children attending all at once. During my first year the oldest pupil was a tall, handsome eleven-year-old called Donald, who lived with his grandmother on an isolated moorland farm. He walked a round trip of fourteen miles every day no matter what the weather: blazing sunshine, driving rain, clinging, swirling sleet and snow.

He was seldom absent and never late; and on winter mornings when the wind howled across the moor to rattle the windows and make the telephone wires sing with a high-pitched hum, arriving at school meant finding Donald thawing his blue, frosted hands in front of the roaring stove in the cloakroom. More often than not his sodden raincoat would be spread across one of the radiators, fed by the cloakroom stove, gently steaming until it was dry again.

His grandmother had an arrangement with the teacher so that a spare shirt, trousers, socks and boots were kept for him in the schoolhouse. If he was soaked through by rain on his seven-mile walk in the early morning he knocked at the schoolhouse door on arrival, was admitted and given his change of clothing. Wet trousers, boots, socks and shirt were then dried out by Miss May during the day to be ready for the morrow should the wet weather persist. As rainfall was high during the autumn and spring and there were few days during the winter when it did not snow, Miss May was kept busy with her drying operations. She never failed Donald on any occasion, not even during prolonged storms, sometimes lasting several days, or even more than a week. She even found time to wash and iron his shirts or do a spot of darning if her judgement decided this was necessary.

As a result Donald's schooling went on uninterrupted by storm and tempest. No matter how wet he became, or chilled by frost and snow, he never seemed to fall foul of flu or colds. Day after day he trudged happily on, fortified by Miss May's kindness and sustained within himself by an inner strength of will which belied his quiet, shy, almost diffident behaviour in class or in the playground. He was the oldest pupil in the school, but never used this to advantage. Unlike a few other boys who came after him he never bullied any of the younger pupils. Instead, he did his best to protect them, boys and girls alike. In doing this he never raised his fists against any troublemaker, merely spoke quietly to the bully who, every time, retreated into a corner to mutter about what he was going to do to Donald when the time was right. But nothing remotely nasty ever happened to Donald. He remained inviolate.

Throughout the eighteen months or so he attended the school while I was there, before going to the academy in Forres, the nearest town, eight miles away, Donald remained wise beyond his years. He was the idol of us younger boys, being everyone's choice as the ideal big brother, and the source of romantic longing from the girls who gazed on his beauty each day and no doubt dreamt wistfully of being hugged by his powerful arms. It saddened us all when Donald left for the secondary school in the town (this meant him having to walk almost six miles from his home to the point on the main road where he could join the school bus at 7.45 every morning).

We had every reason to be sad. He was replaced as oldest pupil by the loud-mouthed, bullying, sadistic son of a forestry worker who wasted no time now that Donald was gone from our midst in spreading his own particular brand of misery. Few escaped his clutches. I knew from the start I would be one of his victims. And I was right. Two years were to elapse before I could exact my revenge. By then I was eight. My tormenter was twelve and almost ready to depart to attempt, no doubt, to cause havoc in the hallowed corridors of the academy.

For two years I saw girls' pigtails savagely pulled by the bully; once he took a pair of scissors and in full view of the gaping occupants of the classroom cut off a huge hank of hair from the head of a girl sitting directly in front. Boys – and girls – were punched for no good reason and if any pupil was foolish enough

to display a bar of toffee or a bag of sweets then the bully moved
in to twist an ear or wrench an arm in order to force the hand-
over of the coveted goods.

Poor Miss Milne, middle-aged and kindly, firm but fair in
dealing with recalcitrant pupils, did her best to control and
curb his activities. She very rarely used the tawse, a strip of
leather about two feet in length and two inches wide with a
shaped handle at the top and several thongs at the other end.
For weeks, sometimes months, it would remain inside her desk,
coiled like a sleeping snake. Most of us were in awe of it; some
were terrified by it. And any time the teacher left the classroom
for several minutes the strap became the object of furtive, hasty
inspections with a crowd of pupils peering beneath the desk lid
as if to check that the monster was still in its lair.

Stamped on the handle was the legend *Made in Lochgelly, Fife,
Scotland.* And on the infrequent occasions when Miss Milne
felt disposed to make use of her ultimate deterrent she would
lift the lid of her desk and always announce to the usually
apprehensive offender, 'You leave me no alternative but to
call my Lochgelly to my aid.' Then she would administer two
sharp cracks, one on each outstretched palm, which left her
slightly breathless and the victim blinking back the tears at the
smarting, tingling, bruising onrush of pain.

To the bully, however, she normally gave two on each hand,
wielding the strap with a force rarely seen at any other time.
On several occasions he moved his hand as the blow was
delivered and the strap cracked viciously across the teacher's
knee. Grinning at her discomfort, he did his best to goad
Miss Milne into losing her temper. He was always denied the
satisfaction of seeing her go out of control. She withstood his
mindless insolence and carried out the punishment no matter
how long it took, perhaps allowing herself the satisfaction of
shoving him away towards his desk when all was done, for the
time being at least.

I suffered, along with the others, a succession of sweet-stealing, shin-kicking, arm-twisting, kidney-punching, hair-pulling incidents which, surprisingly, instead of frightening me into cowed submission nurtured hatred in place of fear. Quietly and grimly I became more determined than ever to get my own back. But I had to bide my time. It had to be done in such a way that no harm would come to me. Much thought went into the planning of my secret revenge; for weeks it absorbed my attention. Once the scheme was ready the dark thoughts that had festered within my mind for so long were clear cut, crystal sharp. I knew exactly what I would do. And how I would do it. And no-one would ever know.

One afternoon as we prepared to leave school at half past three I approached the bully. I told him I knew where there was an old bicycle, in working order, buried in the undergrowth not far from the school. Instead of being surprised by my action he simply accepted what I had to say, no doubt seeing my behaviour as cringing servility. Off we set along the edge of one of the fields I crossed on my journey to and from school. Climbing a fence we entered a wood and reached a path which followed the route taken by a tumbling stream. There was one part, on a bend where the stream gurgled over sharp rocks, in a cleft between sheer, slippery banks fifteen to twenty feet high. The bully followed a few paces behind me, saying nothing, merely whistling between his teeth. When we reached the bend I turned suddenly and with all my force slammed my body into his, knocking him sideways and backwards straight off the narrow path. He disappeared from view, screaming, arms and legs flailing. Then there was silence except for the constant rippling of the water. I did not look over the edge of the bank. Instead, I walked on, only breaking into a run as I left the wood to emerge once again into the full glare of the sun.

At home I carried on with normal, everyday activities. I played with the terrier and had a game with Jack. I ate my tea, showing no apparent signs of having lost my appetite. Once or twice I thought of the screams and the shocked expression on the bully's face. But when I did it was not in fearful recognition of the enormity of what I had done, but to silently gloat at having had the satisfaction of seeing, momentarily, abject terror on the face which had haunted me for almost two weary years. I went to bed at eight o'clock. Outside the sun still shone and woodpigeons murmured softly in the trees surrounding the house. I was still awake when I heard the sound of angry voices in the kitchen. A few minutes later I was summoned by my white-faced mother and emerged with heart thumping to be confronted by my grim-faced father and the father of the bully standing side by side alongside the table.

As I entered the room I was in time to hear the bully's father saying, 'He could easily have killed him – you do realise that?' My father looked even more grim than before. My mother kept shaking her head and picking up and putting down an empty teacup which rattled each time it touched the saucer.

Seemingly, the bully had fallen on to the rocks, gashing his head and knocking himself unconscious. Although parts of his body had been in the water his head had been clear of it so, fortunately, the tragedy of drowning had been averted. Nevertheless his father insisted on several occasions that 'he damn near drowned'. This meant more rattling of teacup and saucer and the blackest look I had ever seen on my father's face. After some time the bully had regained consciousness and crawled over the rocks, going downstream until he reached a place where he could drag himself out and into the wood. He was over two hours late in arriving home from school, exhausted, soaking wet and covered in blood from the head wound. A neighbouring farmer was asked to help and he was taken by car to a doctor in Forres where, his father now repeated several times, 'Six bloody stitches were put in the cut.'

My mother made tea and I was asked if what the bully had

said about events leading up to his fall was true. I made no mention of why I had done it, merely nodded and murmured that indeed it was correct.

'Get back to your bed,' ordered my father.

The bully's father had a liking for whisky. So, too, had my father. Together, they debated the incident over several glasses, in addition to tea and cakes provided by my mother. Gradually, talk of bringing in the police abated as the whisky mellowed the irate father's attitude. I was still awake, pondering my fate, when darkness fell and he left the house to cycle home. But by now he was content to leave all retribution for what had happened to his son in my father's capable hands.

I was never asked what had led me to behave in such a way. I never volunteered the information. It was sufficient for my mother and father merely to know that such a wicked thing had occurred, despite the fact the victim had been a big, strong boy of twelve and their son a puny eight-year-old. Having happened it should never be allowed to happen again. I was beaten on the backside until I thought I would never be able to sit down or lie on my back again. I cried all night and the following day did not fare any better.

At school Miss Milne was ready for me. I was given four of her 'Lochgelly specials' – two on each hand. The punishment was meted out privately during the lunch break when the rest of the school were at play outside. I told her why I had pushed the bully into the stream. Miss Milne was the sort of person to whom the telling of one's troubles came easily. She seemed to understand, but warned me against future futile acts which could lead to tragedy and trouble. After that she never again referred to the incident. The bully was off school for a week. When he returned a lurid scar crossed his forehead and I noticed that one of his front teeth was missing.

What thoughts of revenge simmered in his head I was never to know. But during his remaining few weeks at school he kept his distance and never molested me again. Indeed, he stayed clear of trouble and for the first time for as long as anyone could remember girls came to and went from school with pigtails intact and boys retained their toffee and their self-respect.

During the following winter his father obtained a forestry job in the south of Scotland. Lock, stock and barrel the family moved away and were never seen on the estate again. Several years later the daily newspaper carried a front-page report of a serious car crash near Glasgow. There was also a photograph of the twisted, burnt-out remains. The car had been stolen and when the pursuing police reached what was left of the mangled wreck there was the bully boy crushed behind the steering wheel. He was quite dead.

5

There were no high mountains close to my home, no towering peaks swathed in mist which, with haggis, heather, bagpipes and kilts, are what most foreigners believe Scotland is all about. There was, however, a large curved hill, shaped like an outsize Christmas pudding, a mere pimple really at under 1,500 feet. But to me, as a child, roaming the moors where the curlews cried and the uplands, alive with the bleating of sheep, that hill – the Knock of Braemoray – was my very own mountain, the highest in the land.

The fact that from its summit – a wide plateau of heather and red fescue grass – I could see, miles away on the distant horizon, the snow-encrusted tops of the Cairngorms and the mysterious, brooding presence of the Grampian range did not dampen by one iota my enthusiasm for the hill at my own back door. I gazed at it every day as I went to and from school; from one high classroom window I could even see it as I sat at my desk; in summer with a blue heat haze shimmering above and beyond its upper slopes; in winter coated with snow, glistening and winking in the dying rays of a thin, translucent January sun. And when the mood was on me I would climb to the top, scrambling over boulders, zig-zagging among a labyrinth of peat bogs, thrusting through ankle-deep heather, chest panting and heaving, puffing and blowing, imagining throughout that I was some intrepid explorer or steel-nerved mountaineer.

In 1953, two days after Queen Elizabeth II was crowned in Westminster Abbey and Everest (29,002 feet) had been conquered by Hilary and Tensing (the news reaching Britain on Coronation Day) I went to the summit of the Knock – alone. But in my mind's eye I was followed by lines of porters and teams of heavily laden mules as I headed a breath taking, death-defying expedition. My intention was to plant with due ceremony on the top the flag I had saved from the Coronation Day celebrations.

Once there I opened the old army kit bag I used as a haversack and prepared to unfurl the diminutive Union Jack. Horror. There was no sign of it. In my haste to be off I had forgotten to pack it. However, my mother's thoroughness was much in evidence: a paper bag containing three cheese sandwiches, an apple, a black-skinned banana and a bottle of, by now, dangerously fizzing lemonade. So, I was denied the opportunity of paying homage to the Queen by claiming the Knock of Braemoray as truly a part of her sovereign territory. Instead, I toasted her in what was left of the lemonade after it had foamed all over my face and shoulders when I opened the bottle. I then ate my sandwiches and watched, far below, the tiny specks of occasional cars moving slowly along the main road between the moorland and the low-lying fields and forests.

Several miles distant, on the opposite side, black and grey plumes of smoke drifted lazily into the sky. Whistles blew, echoing eerily across the emptiness which was all around me. Express trains, goods trains, local trains, were labouring up the long, gradual incline on the first haul of their various journeys from the Moray Firth coast through Grantown, Aviemore, Dalwhinnie and on and down to distant Edinburgh, or Glasgow – and beyond.

The sound of their departure for faraway places always fired my imagination; so much so that I spent a considerable amount of time at the railway station watching them come and go. Another favourite vantage point was on top of the high bank beside the massive, many-arched viaduct spanning a gorge through which the river tumbled in a tormented frenzy. Here, on a Sunday afternoon, could be seen the greatest sight of all: the giant express train on its way from Inverness to London with its dozens of carriages hauled by two huge engines, belching smoke and flames, their wheels slipping and slithering on the rails, the thunderous noise of the escaping steam like a sustained protest, ebbing and flowing, as slowly the great weight was hauled higher and higher, up through the surrounding moor. And at the rear, when all the carriages had gone past and there were no more passengers to respond to my enthusiastic arm-waving, the third engine, equally proud and magnificent, pushing the entire train before it, forward and on; on and on and out of sight.

The railway station, along with the post office and shop, was the daily meeting place of many in the district. There was no village, as such, with a neat row of houses on either side of a road. Ours was a scattered community. In the main, houses, farms, land, trees and each and every blade of grass was owned by the estate. The laird, Scottish counterpart of the English squire, was king in this place. And his kingdom was vast. There were thousands of acres: low-lying pastoral land where sleek Aberdeen Angus cattle, heavy and ponderous, were fattened for their beef on the greenest of grass and fields with black, rich loam producing heavy-yielding grain and potato crops; plantations of quick-growing conifers and stately forests of mixed trees (oak, beech, Scots pine and spruce) where pheasants were reared and roe deer, graceful and shy, were sought after so that haunches of venison could grace the laird's dining table; two rivers, with an abundance of salmon and brown trout in every pool; the moorland, where sheep grazed the rough pasture and red grouse were nurtured with loving care, ready to face the much-heralded 12th of August when the shooting season opened and for several weeks each year the air was filled with the cries of men, the barking of dogs and the relentless blasting of shotguns aimed, often haphazardly, at their elusive targets. All this was in the laird's domain.

Those who did not work for the estate were either employed by the tenant farmers on the numerous farms, the railway, the Post Office or the county council. Close to the railway station and beside the main road between Forres and Grantown-on-Spey stood the community hall. The station and hall, the shop, school and church were separated by about half a mile between each place. On beyond the hall was the garage with its two pumps, one for agricultural diesel, one for petrol, both operated by means of a handle laboriously cranked backwards and forwards as each gallon of fuel gushed into the tanks of the waiting vehicles. This was where the bus was kept which on Saturdays ran a regular service throughout the day and evening to Forres and during the week was used as a school bus to take pupils to the secondary school in the town. A further half a mile from the garage stood the blacksmith's shop where the forge glowed red all day long and often far into the night. So, no matter how isolated one's home might be there were daily opportunities for distant neighbour to meet distant neighbour because of the constant traffic of people, walking or cycling (if a farmer, riding in a car), going to and from the various focal points of the community.

The station was one of my favourite places, although the shop came a very close second because of the opportunity to obtain biscuits and sweets, depending on the availability of pocket money and ration coupons (for several years after the Second World War these were still required). In order to reach the railway station I had to go past the shop, so by ensuring that my mother was given the chance of my services to obtain any groceries required, I, in turn, made sure of some pocket money which made a visit to the shop not merely a dream, but a mouth-tingling reality.

The shop was a long, low building beside the main road with a room at one end in which the postmen sorted the mail ready for delivery. A connecting door led to the cottage occupied by the owners. The post office section, with its gleaming brass scales and burnished weights for weighing parcels and outsize letters, was in a corner at the opposite side – at the far end of the broad counter, bleached raw like a sun-dried bone, the result of years of vigorous scrubbing with soap and hot water.

The establishment was run with brisk efficiency by a small, round, jolly woman called Mattie (although we children always referred to her as Miss Robertson, our deferential tone being modified to take account of her mood and the likelihood, or otherwise, of her adding a few extra sweets free when our order was being weighed). She was assisted by Mrs MacGillvray, an elderly aunt, a tall and imposing white-haired figure dressed from head to toe in black.

As my visits to Forres, the nearest town, eight miles away were very rare the shop became a treasure trove of delights to be gazed at and, hopefully, sampled. For a time I became addicted to condensed milk and needed no further bribe from my mother to get me to run an errand to the shop than sufficient money so that I could buy a tin for my own consumption. It was a four-mile round trip between home and shop, along the estate drives, then through a wood of giant pine and larch trees, the twisting path climbing among them, following the banks of a rushing burn in a silent, gloomy, twilight world, the air heavy with the sweet scent of resin.

On the return journey my usual resting place was on a flat rock directly above a waterfall where the burn water cascaded for twenty feet or more down to a round, narrow pool of allegedly awesome depth. It was rumoured to have no exact depth, but to be unfathomable; and in order to keep me from attempting to experiment to try to establish the facts for myself I was told that a kelpie lived there, far beneath the surface of the black water with its perpetual fringe of white scum.

I neither believed nor disbelieved the tale about the kelpie, an evil creature, so I was told, half human, half fish. It did not take me too long to realise that the most awe-inspiring stretches of the two main rivers in the district were all inhabited by kelpies, according to my parents, grandmother and grandfather. If I as much as hinted I might be about to set off to explore such and such a piece of river almost instantly the horror of what could happen if I was seized by a kelpie, should I stray too close to the water's edge, was made graphically clear to me. My grandfather was particularly good on the subject of kelpies, describing with relish, together with vivid hand and arm movements, how the hideous beast could be out of the water in a flash to seize an arm or a leg before dragging the victim behind it back into the pool and far below, never to be seen again. I would only be safe if I kept well back from the water, I was told. Kelpies were unable to travel far on dry land. He even claimed to have known someone – a small boy just like me – who had escaped a kelpie's demented clutch.

'He's the only man who ever made it,' he would tell me. 'Who lived to tell the tale. He's a grown man now, but wears a peg-leg and walks with a crutch. He left his own leg behind him, torn off at the knee, in the kelpie's cave.'

'Could I meet him?' I asked. I always asked this question when my grandfather got going on this particular story.

'Oh no,' he always replied. 'He lives too far away now for us to visit him.'

I wondered. There was a man in Forres who looked after the car park, emerging now and then from a little green hut in the town square. He had a peg-leg and stomped about the town on a crutch, the wooden leg clumping on the pavement. Until I first heard the kelpie story from my grandfather's lips I believed the man to be a former pirate – now retired. My parents thought differently. They said he had been a soldier in the First World War and had been wounded in a battle called the Somme. I didn't think much of their explanation, He definitely had the look of a pirate about him. But my grandfather made me reflect on this theory. Could he be the sole survivor of an attack by a kelpie? For years I wanted to ask him. Once I even approached him. But my courage failed me when I heard him swearing in a deep, gruff voice at a dog caught peeing against the side of his hut. So, at the last minute, I turned away, my question unasked.

Such was my nature that all this talk of kelpies, the descriptions of their awful and horrifying appearance, the sheer unadulterated terror they were capable of inflicting on anyone who set eyes on them, only served to make me more curious than ever. Instead of keeping a safe distance away from those dangerous parts of the river said to be inhabited by them, I would creep, heart pounding, mouth dry, right to the extreme edge of the bank. And there I would lie on my stomach gazing down at the pool, watching with eyes on stalks, hardly daring to breathe, waiting for that moment often terrifyingly described by my grandfather when the kelpie would break through the surface and search with piercing eyes the surroundings for any signs of prey. But no kelpie ever materialised from the depths of the black, foam-churned water. And, surprisingly enough, I never fell into the river.

So, there above the waterfall on the Poldo Burn, high above the black pit wherein yet another kelpie lurked in sinister splendour, I would sit myself down and from my mother's shopping basket produce my personal tin of condensed milk. I opened the tin with the Scout knife I carried on my belt and from a pocket in my shorts emerged the teaspoon that always accompanied me on expeditions to the shop. Scooping and swallowing the rich, thick mess contained in the tin took all my attention, so great was my taste for the stuff. Working my way through the contents and feeling slightly sick by the time I reached the bottom, I was oblivious of practically everything going on around me: the dipper nesting in a cleft in the rock behind the wall of spray; the wagtails and thrushes alighting to drink from the shallows above the waterfall; the woodpeckers that nested year after year in a decaying tree close to the footbridge downstream from where I sat.

While I slurped and savoured my way through the gooey contents of the tin nothing else was of any consequence. If the kelpie had wanted to choose an instant to catch me completely off guard, then half way through my tin of condensed milk would have been the best moment in which to strike. And I'm sure had he done so my first reaction would not have been one of terror, but frustration that I had not been given sufficient time to finish the lot.

At the shop a bell tinkled merrily whenever the door was opened and you entered to be greeted by a delicious smell compounded of cheese, lentils, oatmeal, sealing wax and soap. Along the full length of the wall behind the counter were several shelves and two rows of drawers, each with a white porcelain knob and a neatly lettered label signifying the contents: *Split Peas, Raisins, Sultanas, Currants, Sugar, Tea, Rice, Cream of Tartar, Barley, Lentils, Salt.* The shelves held a glorious mixture of goods ranging from bottles of Camp coffee and jars of jam and marmalade to tins of Kiwi shoe polish and bottles of bleach. Here and there among the bottles and tins were displayed neat piles of shoelaces, brown and black, and thick, dark bootlaces, like art exhibits providing relief from the more mundane everyday objects waiting to be sold. A cardboard box containing candles was at one end of the counter and a huge round cheese stood resplendently on a marble slab. It was always the same kind – yellow, standard mousetrap – and when a portion was required either Mattie or Mrs MacGillvray cut it free with a thin wire, then weighed the section on shining brass scales (a larger version of those used in the post office part of the shop), retaining or rejecting the round, polished weights until the two sides balanced perfectly. Sugar was scooped from one of the drawers and poured into a stout, brown bag to be weighed in the same fashion. And such was the two women's dexterity with the scales that vast quantities of various loose items, such as rice, barley, salt and oatmeal, could be bagged and weighed with hardly a pause.

Having handed over my mother's shopping list I would stand and gaze at the sweets as the items were prepared and placed on the counter. There were usually no more than six or seven large jars of assorted sweets from which to choose, but to me it was a vast array requiring careful thought before a final decision was reached. Value for money was also a key factor in decision making, often taking precedence over taste.

Humbugs in one jar, mixed boilings in another, huge white Imperial mints, which we called pandrops; Sharp's toffees and caramels, chocolates (too expensive), liquorice allsorts and fruit drops; a bewildering kaleidoscope of reds and greens, purples and yellows. There were also thick slabs of toffee (combining taste and longevity) wrapped in greaseproof paper with a drawing of a Highland cow, shaggy-haired and long-horned, on the front. This was my favourite of all the sweets: McCowan's Highland Toffee, so chewy that your teeth and jaws ached with the effort of breaking it down. The same firm's liquorice toffee, long and black with a thick white centre, was also much in demand and if twopence was all I had then there was no decision to make, beyond whether it be a slab of Highland Toffee or liquorice toffee. I also liked Mars bars, but they were dearer and in my pecking order of priority concerning confectionery classed as a luxury.

But the days when my mind raced, becoming more confused as the minutes ticked by and my face broke into a flush, were those when I had more than twopence to spend and a quarter pound of one of the range from the jars came within reach. Sometimes the kindly Mattie solved my dilemma by selecting a few from each jar until the weight of four ounces was reached. She then added a couple for luck, smiled, and charged me the price of the cheapest on display; and I ran from the shop and into the sunlight clutching my treasure as if it were a consignment of precious jewels. The contents of the bag might have to last me for several days. So, I became a hoarder, a veritable squirrel of a boy, measuring my wealth in the way that a bedouin Arab covets camels and goats. Only in my case the riches took the form of tongue-tingling pandrop mints and slab after slab of delicious tooth-shattering, jaw-breaking, mouth-aching manna from Heaven, McCowan's Highland Toffee.

6

At the railway station the station master was a pandrop addict. His devotion to the round, white mints was legendary and known throughout the district. A visit to the station to collect a crate or a package or to buy a ticket for a journey often resulted in a gift of his favourite sweets being made. Tricks were played on him, which he vastly enjoyed. Once, on a coach outing to the seaside with school pupils and other parents, he asked someone to buy him a few sweets when we stopped for a break in a town. Back came the sweets, fourteen pounds of pandrops, rattling and rustling inside a large, thick brown paper bag. And adults and children alike laughed for the rest of the day as he carried it with him wherever we went; even down to the beach.

A large glass jar of pandrops stood on the window sill beside his desk and all who entered, whether on business to arrange the carriage of sheep or cattle away to market, to buy a ticket or merely for a gossip in front of the permanently glowing coal fire, were offered a sweet. Few refused. Certainly, I never did. Pandrops came in two sizes: small – and manageable – and extra large. The station master's preference was for the giant variety. It was possible, with care, to make one last for a full hour. Conversation was, of course, difficult in the initial stages, but I soon learned the trick of tucking the pandrop into my cheek (as he did) and talking without hindrance while enjoying the feast. I used to marvel at his skill in speaking on the telephone should it ring just after he had popped one of the large white sweets into his mouth. He had a round, moon-like face with bushy eyebrows and cheeks polished like two red apples. With his reading glasses on he resembled a benevolent owl. With a pandrop jammed firmly into the side of his mouth his cheeks bulged and he became a hamster storing food in a pouch.

The railway station was truly a place of wonder and excitement. It straddled a busy line taking passenger and goods trains to and from Inverness and the south. As the railway was single track the station had two sets of lines so that 'up' trains and 'down' trains could pass each other. This meant there were many occasions throughout the day when trains would be at one side or the other awaiting the arrival of the one that had priority. There were all sorts of trains to watch, and plenty of them: from expresses hauled by streamlined, gleaming engines painted black, red and green, emblazoned with names like *The Highlander, Waverley,* and *Rob Roy MacGregor,* displaying shining coats of arms, some of which thundered through without stopping amid a maelstrom of whistle-blowing and rushing wind; to high funnelled, workmanlike, crawling engines, belching smoke and red-hot cinders, hauling endless lines of clanking waggons. Loads of coal and fertiliser, bleating sheep, cattle wide-eyed with fright and bellowing, and cargoes of mystery and intrigue hidden under vast tarpaulins with the word *Danger* proclaimed in enormous white letters on either side; all these rumbled past my enthralled and prying eyes.

I was fascinated by the railwaymen's language, puzzled at first by their references to 'down' trains which climbed the gradient – but went south – and 'up' trains which clattered past going downhill towards Forres – but went north. A wooden signal box, reached by a long flight of steps on the outside, stood at either end of the vast length of cinder-strewn platform. The station buildings were almost in the centre with, on the opposite side and reached by a footbridge, a small building with two doors marked *Ladies' Waiting Room* and *Gentlemen's Waiting*

Room. There was a covered section with no door between the two rooms with posters featuring smiling adults and laughing, sandcastle-building children on the walls. There were names like Skegness, the Isle of Arran, Gourock, Rothesay and Clacton-on-Sea printed on them. I gazed at them all as if they were exotic places in far-off lands. A narrow bench, painted chocolate brown, sat inside, facing the platform. Of course, no-one ever waited in any of them or in their counterparts, similarly designated, in the main station building. If you were waiting you did so in the main office, which had *Station Master* printed on the door, while you sampled one of his pandrops and warmed yourself in front of the fire.

Sometimes if the laird had guests arriving or departing a fire would be lit in one of the waiting rooms. Mostly, this was a mere formality. Like us lesser mortals, fur-laden ladies and gents with large moustaches and highly checked knickerbocker suits, surrounded by fishing rods and shotguns and pile upon pile of expensive-looking luggage, usually ended up in front of the station master's fire. There they warmed their bottoms or their knees, basking in the heat, rejecting or accepting the inevitable pandrop and, occasionally, if a train was running particularly late, sipping a cup of tea made by the station master's wife in the house on the other side of the wall.

There were three men working with the station master and apart from a few hours around midnight the four were on duty, in shifts, throughout the day. They lived in a long row of cottages on a slope above the track, with the gardens running downhill to the fence on a bank alongside the line. There were eight cottages in the row, all of them occupied by railwaymen – those employed in the station and the men who worked on maintaining the track, out in all weather tramping through sleet and snow, sunshine and rain with barrow, shovel and hammer for testing the soundness of bolts fastening rail to sleeper. In railway language the track was called the 'permanent way'; the workmen were referred to as 'P-way' men. I loved that name. It had a jolly, carefree comic book ring to it.

During slack periods between trains it was not unusual to find the station deserted, but everyone knew they would be able to find whoever was on duty in his garden, hoeing or planting, digging potatoes, or tying-in the new crop of raspberry canes. They were all keen gardeners, the station master included, and the interest they took in their own plots, with their displays of colourful flowers and neat rows of vegetables, was reflected in the general appearance of the railway premises.

Away from the immediate surrounds of the buildings the lengthy platforms with their covering of cinders were regularly hoed and kept weed-free; and on the grass banks flower beds offered tantalising splashes of multicoloured lupins, hollyhocks, delphiniums, sweet williams, marigolds and rich, heady, sweet-scented stock. Nasturtiums – both giant and 'Tom Thumb' – climbed and crawled in a trembling, waving, shaking canopy over every fence, in one spot covering the entire roof of a small shed used for the storage of spare hurricane lamps and warning detonators. The name of the station was there for all to see, the letters formed by neatly arranged clumps of bedding plants chosen to provide continuous flowering throughout the summer and autumn; and at the door entering on to the platform two massive tractor tyres, painted white, were laid on either side. The space inside each one was filled with earth to produce year after year a profusion of scents and colours from snowdrops and daffodils in the spring to lobelia, wallflowers and aubretia for the rest of the growing season.

There was great excitement each year as the time for the judging of the 'Best Maintained Station' came round. But there was never any need for hasty, last-minute painting, weeding and window-cleaning to be done. The station was always in apple-pie order, both inside and out, and invariably station master and staff were given first prize; if not they were always second. Their main rival was the tiny moorland station at Dava six miles away in the direction of Grantown-on-Spey. Competition was fierce. A close watch, through a network of spying engine drivers, firemen and guards and local farmers, was kept on the rival's progress throughout the year.

If at some stage it appeared that superiority might not be maintained in the annual competition startling innovations made an appearance in the floral displays in order to win the judges' approval. The head gardener at the Big House would come to the rescue with a new species of shrub or someone like my father, who enjoyed gardening and with whom sweet peas were his crowning glory, would lend a hand in order that local honour could be satisfied. So great was the show of high, handsome sweet peas, rich in scent and bloom, that the first year they were grown in a long line trained to felled birch saplings staked alongside one of the platforms, passengers alighted to admire them during the waiting time while the engine's water tanks were being replenished. The sweet pea plants were eight to ten feet high, each one with massive flowers, the entire display intertwined among the branches of the saplings. It was a masterstroke. That year, at least, the station came top. Next year the rival achieved amazing things with begonias in pots and a miniature flower clock modelled on the one in Edinburgh's Princes Street Gardens. Our station reluctantly gave up the coveted scroll, at the same time planning secretly how best to wrest it away again the following year. Which we did.

The station master's office was, in reality, the booking office, but no member of the public had ever to wait at the hatch in the wall in order to buy a ticket. You entered a long, high, narrow room festooned with cut flowers in a variety of vases and jam jars, to hear the whirring and pinging of the two machines (Tyler's Patent Train Tablet Apparatus) which kept the staff informed of trains entering and leaving the section of track under their control; to see a coal fire glowing, even

on the warmest summer day; to sniff at the air heavy with pipe
tobacco smoke, intermingled with the delicate perfume of the
various flowers and the raw, metallic bite of the oil from the
mechanism of the three large levers which operated the points
on the two sets of lines within the station and at the junction
to the shunting and goods sidings a short distance away. A
longcase wall clock hung over the fireplace, the brass pendulum
swinging slowly from side to side behind the glass-fronted door.
The rhythmic, ponderous 'tick-tock, tick-tock' of the movement
dominated the silence when voices were stilled as pipes were
being filled, and for a few moments at least the friendly banter
and conversations about crops and cattle and sheep and the
general run-down state of the minister's garden at the manse
would cease in a reflective interlude of drowsy contentment.

Tyler's Patent Train Tablet Apparatus consisted of a matching
pair of machines in a highly polished light-brown wood – one for
the 'up' line and the other for the 'down' line. They contained
flat and key-shaped tokens made of copper brass, the surfaces
worn smooth by many years of use. As this was a single-track
railway no driver was allowed to set off along any part of it until
a token was released by the machine, which had been activated
by the next signalman along the line. This was then placed in
a leather pouch and the entire thing, called a tablet, handed
over by one of the station staff. On arrival at the next station
the tablet was handed back by the engine driver and a fresh
one obtained for the next section of his journey. Whenever a
train left Forres on the 'down' line or Dava on the 'up', the
particular machine would clatter and ping, make a series of
whirring noises then fall silent. It was now time for a lever to
be pulled and there was the token ready for use, the others
visible behind a small glass screen, still locked into position.
As each one came forward it left a space at the rear into which
the token received was inserted, thus alerting the next station
that the train was on its way.

When an express train was going through without stopping the tablet was attached to a circular frame of wire covered by tough cloth. The station master stood on the platform, close to the edge, facing the oncoming train now slowing down for its run through the station, the tablet held up and out in his right hand. His left arm was also outstretched, the wrist bent so that like a hoopla ring the engine driver could drop his tablet over the waiting wrist. Never once did I see the tablets miss their target. Both were always expertly caught by both driver and station master who then turned away out of the rushing wind caused by the passage of the moving train.

If the train involved was one of the really high-speed expresses, or one that was trying to make up lost time, then the tablet with token pouch attached was fixed to a catching apparatus on the signal gantry alongside the line. As the engine raced past a similar device on the side of the driving cab caught the waiting tablet and slammed a counterpart into a ready-primed catch which crashed shut and held it.

To see a high-speed express, travelling on the 'up' line going downhill to Forres, from the platform only a few feet away was a thrill beyond measure. First there was the whistling when the train was in a deep cutting between the school and the shop; next, the sight of it rounding the bend where the signal box stood, the whistle-blowing growing more urgent, one blast followed directly by another, the noise of the wheels and the hiss of steam becoming a roar as it swept towards the station buildings and the figures watching from the platform in front of the door. Everything was a blur as it went past, engine and carriages, a few faces looking out, the noise like a sustained roll of thunder, above it all the whistle now sounding in one long and final cry like an awful scream, trailing away into oblivion as the end carriage disappeared from view under the road bridge; and all that was left was the 'clackety-clack, clackety-clack' of the departing wheels growing fainter until once more you could hear the birds calling and the cattle lowing in a nearby field and the whirring of the token machine inside the station; and the voice of someone invariably remarking with a thoughtful shake of the head,

'My God, yon bugger's in a hurry thé day.'

While a fascinating place by day, the railway station took on an added dimension of mystery and adventure at night, especially in the winter months. In 1951 when mains electricity was brought to all the houses in the district (not just those at the side of the road) the station, however, continued to be lit, both inside and out, by paraffin lamps. A hissing, spluttering Tilley stood permanently on the ledge above the station master's desk, while the rest of the room was lit by hurricane lamps. Similar lamps provided light in the hallway where the massive weighing machine stood alongside the door and on the platform several were suspended beneath the canopy directly in front of the main building. Hurricane lanterns were also used by the staff while going about their various tasks – crossing to the opposite platform, cycling to the signal boxes at either end, shepherding passengers from the bright lights of the train through the dark to where a friend or relative usually waited in the office.

The sight of an express train running through at high speed in the middle of a storm at night, with, perhaps, a gale blowing and snow-filled clouds scudding across the face of the moon, was the ultimate thrill: the hurricane lamps on their hooks, swaying in the wind; the black, distorted shadows writhing and twisting as the lights moved to and fro; the figures huddled together, watching, in the shelter of the canopy over the door. Then – the sound of the whistle half a mile away, growing louder, eerie and sinister because of the surrounding darkness; the shape of the engine outlined behind the weak, white light on its front; the deafening noise, then the roar; the blur of carriage lights; and the rattle of the departing wheels, the red lamp at the rear fading to the size of a glowing cigarette butt; then vanishing.

I watched them go by and each time my heart pounded, a response to the thrill engendered by the raw, naked power I had witnessed; and the knowledge that secretly I wanted to be out there, on the train, hurtling into the unknown through the blackness of the night.

Despite the remoteness of the locality the station was a busy place for much of the year. Although the school bus ran to Forres in the mornings and back again in the afternoons, apart from Saturdays when a regular service was available, there was no other way to reach the town during the week than by train. And there were plenty of those – in both directions – throughout the day, many of them expresses which had come from Edinburgh, Glasgow or London, bound for Inverness, or were heading away from there on the journey to the south.

It was also possible, if an urgent visit was required to the doctor or dentist in the town, to be stowed away in the little covered waggon serving as the guard's van on a goods train. Although I loved travelling in this fashion my mother was never particularly keen, due partly to the element of discomfort involved. There was no seat in the van, apart from a small, hard bench for the guard, but she never complained if the opportunity arose for us to clamber aboard after arriving at the station. She appreciated that we were being granted a special privilege and repaid the guard's generosity in full by plying him with sweets or, later, ensuring that a rabbit or a brace of wood pigeon was left at the station to be given to him on his next journey through.

I enjoyed travelling in the guard's van on the goods trains so much that, really, I never wanted to travel the proper way, in a seat in a proper carriage. There was a strong aura of wild adventure in the sight of the high-sided, flat-roofed, dingy brown van, with its tall chimney and open platform, with railed sides, front and rear. Inside a fire glowed in a round-bellied stove and there was sometimes a mug of tea to be had from a kettle newly boiled on its top. The highlight of the journey was to be allowed to stand with the guard on the platform at the rear while my mother sat on his bench beside the stove. Here, I could clutch the safety rail tightly and look back at the receding countryside, my imagination telling me I was in America rattling my way through Indian country on a railroad crossing the wild and woolly west. The farmers' cattle, grazing contentedly in the lush grass of the fields beside the track, became herds of maddened buffalo about to stampede; and each time we came to a bumping, juddering, clanking halt (as goods trains were prone to do on various sections of the line) I waited for the 'thwack' and the 'thud' of the arrows and the answering fire of Winchester repeaters; then, at the last minute, as we all faced scalping and death from the upraised tomahawks, the bugles and drumming hooves of the US cavalry charging to the rescue across the open plains.

There was also the excitement of alighting from the waggon and on to the cinders beside the track at a signal box on the outskirts of the town. Because this was not an 'officially approved' means of travelling on the railway this kept everyone safe from any prying eyes within the large station in Forres. Once our feet were safely on the ground the train would slowly ease away, couplings clanking and banging, the guard waving from the doorway. I used to wave back enthusiastically, full of envy and longing, as if he were bound for some distant foreign country in his little brown van with the smoking chimney. 'What a life,' I would think aloud until my mother dragged at my arm and hauled me behind her up the grassy bank and on to the bridge over which ran the road going into the town.

There was always an element of haste, something distinctively furtive, in my mother's impatient behaviour at this stage in the proceedings; I expect because of the nature of our unorthodox arrival in the town. I absorbed this sense of guilt and determined urgency to the full. Once more my imaginative apparatus started whirring. Now, the Wild West was behind me. And as I slipped through the massed ranks of shoulder-high cow parsley and tall, waving grass and clambered over the roadside fence behind my mother I was transformed into the role of secret agent newly arrived clandestinely in German-occupied France. Once across the bridge I would be met by a member of the Resistance. Was that him? The road sweeper, with the drooping shoulder and cruelly bent back, wielding his broom on the pavement near the bend where the road curved at the foot of the hill and the first of the town's buildings came into view? Was that black car coming towards us full of Gestapo officers in search of a new torture victim? Were there snipers on the roof of the mill beside the river where they ground corn into porridge oats and as far as I could see (and taste) left as many husks in the bags as they did pure oats? Within seconds I was firmly in the grip of a new adventure. I skulked close to the fence, eyes darting this way and that, trailing behind my mother as she strode purposefully on into town, more relaxed now that the railway line was behind her, as she walked consulting shopping lists, checking and rechecking the contents of her purse.

'Hurry up,' she would turn her head and shout. 'You've not got all day, you know. I've plenty to do.'

But in one respect she was wrong. I did have all day in which to indulge my fantasies; all day and indeed every day; all the time in the world. And not even trailing in and out of the butcher's, the baker's, the ironmonger's, the fish shop, the newsagent's and the greengrocer's; or waiting for what seemed like hours in the doctor's waiting-room or the palm-clenching, sweat-drenching, fear-laden atmosphere of the dentist's surgery, could dislodge the world of make-believe from my inner being. For me the small market town became the world's most wicked city; and throughout the time I was there on each and every visit I kept one step ahead of death and waited for danger at the corner of every narrow street.

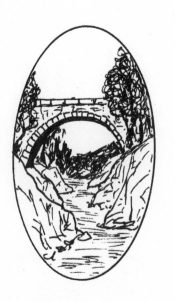

7

My maternal grandfather, a tall hawk-nosed man with a shock of fine, fiery-red hair, was known locally as 'The Red Terror'. This was not so much for his skill in apprehending poachers on the estate where he was head gamekeeper, but because of the highly unorthodox methods which he used in order to achieve success. As a result of his legendary exploits, always tinged with an element of fun, due to his own highly developed sense of humour, someone invented a new salmon fly and named it after him. As a lure for enticing salmon 'The Red Terror' was every bit as deadly and successful as the man who gave it its name.

One evening, having found a local worthy fishing for salmon in one of the best pools on the river, my grandfather, who for evermore I called Ginga because of my inability to pronounce the word 'Grandad', hid himself in a thicket of trees to watch the man enjoying to the full his illicit sport. Recognising the individual as a persistent offender he was content to wait until dusk began to settle over the forest on either bank of the rushing river. The poacher fished on amid the silent gloom, unaware of the eyes of his arch-enemy following his every move, watching not only to see if a salmon was hooked, but patiently waiting until the time was ripe to give the maximum impact to the ploy he had in mind.

The moment came when the moon started to show its face beyond the brooding canopy of the trees and deep patches of shadow lurked among the rocks and the bushes overhanging the bank. Lifting his double-barrelled twelve-bore shotgun to his shoulder, Ginga loosed off a shot which demolished the point of the poacher's fishing rod as he raised it in the air in order to cast the line once more across the dark water of the silent pool. He then fired the second barrel into the air above the poacher's head, the noise of both shots sending roosting pheasants and wood pigeons clattering through the trees, amid a babble of screeching and squawking from similarly alarmed magpies and jays.

The startled poacher added his screams to the noise and confusion and dropped the rod into the pool. Within seconds the turbulent current had borne the broken parts away downstream. He made no attempt to retrieve them. He was already running as if pursued by the most fiendish of demons, leaping over boulders, scrambling up the steep bank, forcing a terrified passage through nettles, bracken and tangled barriers of bramble until he reached the woodland path. Once there he was off at the gallop, with never a backward glance, while Ginga, chortling and chuckling and clutching his sides, clambered down to the river's edge to remove the man's bag, containing flies, hooks and other accessories, from the branch of a tree close to the pool.

Next day, while the man was at work on a nearby farm and his wife had gone to the village shop, Ginga left the bag, with fishing tackle intact, on the front doorstep of the poacher's cottage. But the fishing reel, from the shot-blasted rod, he kept for himself as a spoil of war, after having salvaged it from the river. A search found the broken pieces of rod jammed between two large rocks several hundred yards downstream. In due course the farm worker saved enough money to buy himself another rod and reel, but he never again went poaching on Ginga's domain.

My grandfather used to see him cycling along the road with the sections of the rod in their case tied to the crossbar of the bicycle. They would wave to each other across the low stone wall surrounding Ginga's garden. Sometimes, they would pass the time of day at this and on other occasions when they met. But fish or fishing was never mentioned – by either side. So long as the poacher went elsewhere to someone else's territory for a spell of illegal fishing Ginga was perfectly happy. It was then up to some other person to pit his wits against those of the inveterate poacher.

All the same Ginga was never forgiven by the poacher's wife for the fear he had caused her husband that fateful night when twin shots shattered the silence and sent him fleeing in panic back to her bed. From that day on she refused to speak to my grandfather, although remaining on the best of terms with Granny. Obviously it satisfied her immensely to behave in this fashion because the one-sided feud was carried on in silence over many years. So great was its strength that she once pointedly ignored Ginga when, due to a quirk of fate, they found themselves next to each other as arms were being linked for the singing of 'Auld Lang Syne' at a New Year's dance in the village hall.

'Never,' she shouted above the music and laughter and general din, tearing herself free from his enthusiastic clutch. Rushing to the other side of the room she faced him in stony silence as the twin lines of interlinked merrymakers, arms around each other's waists, danced up to and away from each other, backwards and forwards. Ginga laughed and blew her a kiss, while her husband shook his head and smiled at the depths of loyalty inherent in the woman he had married.

Grandpa and Granny Macgregor lived about five miles from us on a neighbouring estate. This was the estate on which my father had been working when he met my mother, one of a family of three daughters. Before he was provided with a small van – grandly described as a shooting brake because of its windows and panels of wood on its sides – so that he could get around the estate more easily, he went everywhere, along the paths on the river banks, up and down the drives and moorland tracks, by bicycle. And this was how, from time to time, we would travel whenever visiting my mother's parents in their cottage on a grassy knoll high above a curving gorge where the River Findhorn thundered over the rocks in a perpetual cloud of misty spray. Pine, spruce and larch trees clung like limpets to the steep, almost vertical bank falling away from the drying-green at the back door. Both inside the house and out the distant roaring and rumbling of the river dominated all other sounds; and when in full spate after a winter's storm it was possible from the drying-green to look down and see, far below, a seething, boiling cauldron of foam and water, black as ink, with the spray rising slowly through the trees like some cloud of smoke released from the lair of a dragon.

Before I was old enough to ride a bicycle I was carried on a seat fastened to the crossbar of my father's cycle. Off we would set, father, mother and son on two bicycles, with Jack flying along above us, screeching and cackling incessantly, swooping down from time to time to alight on the handlebars when hills were reached and it was time to walk. Another participant in those journeys to visit my grandparents was Chuffy, our pet cairn terrier.

When my father was released from the army after the war he was given, in common with other local men who had been away in the Forces, a small sum of money raised by the district 'Welcome Home' committee. Whist drives, sales of works, impromptu concerts in the hall – all had contributed to the coffers of the 'Welcome Home Fund'. So, with his share, my father purchased Chuffy, then a small puppy (named by me after a little dog who lived in a barrel in a favourite picture book of mine), and a portable wireless set with, wonder of wonders, a 'dry' battery. Thus was ended for ever the drudgery of having 'wet' accumulators taken to and brought back from the town where they were recharged ready for further use in the backroom of a cycle repair shop.

For a time, when she was tiny, Chuffy made the journeys to my grandparents' sitting in a wicker basket fastened to the handlebars of my mother's bicycle, reclining in regal splendour with her two front paws resting on the edge, head swivelling from side to side as she surveyed the passing scenery, barking volubly should a rabbit dash across the road in front of us. When she grew older she was allowed to run alongside the bicycles while we were on the estate drives. This part of the proceedings she loved more than any other, racing along, four little legs moving in blurred harmony, pink tongue lolling. From time to time she allowed herself the luxury of investigating strange scents on the grassy verge of the roads, even plunging out of sight into hedges and woods in pursuit of elusive rabbits. Halting to call her back was of no use. She ignored even my father's brisk, authoritative commands. She had a mind of her own and she let everyone know it. But as soon as we had cycled away and she thought she was going to be abandoned out she would pop from the undergrowth, barking with grim determination, to pursue us relentlessly, head lowered and cocked to one side.

Because we lived in a valley, and due to the situation of his cottage, whichever of three possible routes we took to get to Ginga's house involved either climbing or descending a series of steep hills. One of the steepest, and by far the most alarming, was over a mile and a half long. It came to a finish after a number of hairpin bends on a narrow, hump-backed, stone-walled bridge beneath which ran the River Findhorn in a rock-strewn ravine more than one hundred feet below. Once across, the road climbed away again almost as steeply through a damp, shadow-filled wood to emerge on a narrow plateau of land with fields, a farm, my grandparents' cottage and, beyond, yet more wood-covered hills.

This road with its hairpin bends, the first of which snaked round at right angles from the parapet of the bridge, before the hill, known as the Daltullich Brae, went abruptly into a 1 in 3 gradient, was the main reason why my grandparents' visits to us were extremely rare. Ginga, who owned a small, blue Hillman saloon, positively refused to drive up it except when some dire emergency occurred, or Granny made his life a misery until he was forced to agree in order to end hostilities.

The reason for this was his inability to change gear with any certainty while the car was toiling up such a desperate slope; and his total inability to move the car forward again if the worst came to the worst and they came to a complete halt. It was, most certainly, the most fearsome hill in the district – and the most dangerous. To ascend, then stall at one of the tight bends, and find oneself going backwards instead of up, was alarming in the extreme, the fear and tension being heightened by the knowledge of the hundred-foot drop into the river when the bridge was reached. Descending with Ginga at the wheel was almost as horrifying, but in this case he crawled down the full mile and a half in first gear with his foot held firmly on the brake pedal, the handbrake gripped in one hand – and locked partially on. The brakes never failed him, although from time to time they smoked a great deal and the sickening stench of burning rubber filled the car.

If for some reason he was absolutely forced into making the ascent then Granny had to pay penance for her persistence in nagging him into doing something much against his will; for tempting providence by compelling him to put his fate into the lap of the gods. At the foot of the hill running down from their cottage he would halt the car and get into first gear. Then, with a lurch, off he would go, over the hump in the bridge and round and into the first bend. By now, due to his low speed, the engine would be straining and both Granny and he would be hunched forward in their seats, willing the old car forward.

From the right-hand bend the road rose abruptly, then veered away to the left at the second tight corner. It was here that Ginga always came unstuck. With the engine screaming in protest the car had insufficient speed and power to cope with the gradient increasing dramatically on such a sharp bend and here, with a grinding lurch, would come to a halt, usually with the engine stalled. There, on the 1 in 3 slope, the little Hillman clung like an unwelcome fly, Ginga with the brake pedal hard on the floor and the handbrake pulled up as far as the lever would go. To be in the back seat was a terrifying experience. There being no rear doors and forced to peer in terror at the slope behind through the narrow back window instantly brought on mixed fears of both vertigo and claustrophobia.

'Get out, woman, and put a stone behind the wheels,' Ginga would roar at Granny, already struggling to open the door. The very first occasion she made the ascent must have been an arduous one for her finding big enough stones on the banks of the road which would fit behind the rear wheels. But by now she was remarkably adept and knew exactly where to go. Scrambling into the grass she would emerge clutching a rock in both hands and place it at the rear, pushing and prodding until it was jammed firmly against a wheel. Sometimes two were required, one for each wheel; sometimes they were not large enough, with insufficient weight to hold the car; sometimes too round and instead of holding firm against the tyres would roll off down the hill, leaving Granny shrieking and Ginga yelling that he couldn't hold the bloody thing back much longer and would she hurry up and do something about it. Puffing and panting from her exertions, Granny would hurry to and fro in her search for suitable rocks until at last she felt confident enough to announce that the task was accomplished: the car was firmly anchored on the hill.

Now Ginga was free to remove a white-knuckled hand from the brake lever. Granny had to stand by on the road in case of any further last-minute mishap. He would then get the engine started again, fight with the bucking gear lever until with a series of shattering crunches first gear was engaged once more, yell to Granny to climb aboard and release the handbrake. For a fraction of a second the Hillman would rock gently against the stones at the rear, then lurch forward like some overweight beetle while Granny struggled to get her door shut and Ginga leaned forward on the edge of his seat, teeth clenched tightly on the stem of his pipe while mouthing, 'Come on, come on,' foot stabbing and jabbing at the accelerator pedal.

Lurching and heaving, the tiny car toiled into and around the second bend, but invariably as soon as its nose was sent into the savage right-hand curve of bend number three it would stall once again on the hideous slope. Granny's performance with the roadside rocks would then be repeated amid the same tense air of disaster about to strike; and when, eventually, the mission was accomplished off they would go again, leaving yet another pile of stones in the middle of the road to mark the progress of their ascent.

The hill then climbed nearly as steeply, but in a straight line, for a further three-quarters of a mile where it crossed a major road. Ginga never stopped here, but always sent the Hillman full pelt across the junction in order to have sufficient power to get round yet another hairpin bend, where the road snaked to the right to run through a small village with the houses clinging to the steep banks on either side. At the far end of the street was the last bend, hard round to the left, and still on a horrifying slope; then, only one hundred yards were left before flat countryside was reached.

For the first time since leaving home Granny could relax with the crest of the awful hill now in sight. With trembling fingers she would reach over to where I cowered on the back seat and hand me a toffee. Ginga, equally white-faced, was now by this time searching for second gear, giving a grunt of satisfaction when, at last, the cogs and wheels ceased to scream and meshed in the proper place. Bowling forward at twenty miles per hour it was a matter of little consequence whether or not Ginga engaged third – or top – gear. Sometimes he tried – and failed; sometimes, tired by his efforts on the hill, he didn't even bother to attempt the task. And so, they would complete the remaining three miles of the journey to my home with the car in second gear. Long after I was back in the house the straining, screaming protests of the tortured engine and gearbox would live on inside my head; and I would wake in the middle of the night from wild dreams of tumbling through emptiness while trapped on the Hillman's rear seat. I always gained consciousness just before the inevitable plunge beneath the surface of the river was reached.

Ginga had never received any driving lessons. In the early 1930s he obtained his first – and only – car, climbed in behind the steering wheel, and drove off. No driving test was necessary; a licence was granted automatically upon application. To drive with him, even without the drama of a hill to negotiate, was an adventure surpassing all other adventures.

Now and then I spent holidays with my grandparents, the highlight of which was a twelve-mile journey to Nairn, on the Moray Firth coast, so that Granny could do a large shopping. It would have been nearer to have gone to Forres, but as this route involved negotiating the dreaded Daltullich Brae, and shopping expeditions were not considered to be either emergencies or legitimate reasons for Granny's wrath, Ginga's refusal on this score to point the Hillman in that direction was tolerated for as long as they lived in their home above the river, a total of forty-one years.

An outing to Nairn began, first of all, by Granny announcing a day or two in advance that she had to go into town that week. Ginga's initial reaction, on every occasion, was to plead pressure of work; he was far too busy feeding pheasant chicks, controlling vermin, shooting rabbits, organising the salmon fishing (depending on the season of the year he always had a cast-iron excuse) to take time off to waste, so he said, on taking her to town. The subject would then be broached again and again at mealtimes in the face of continuing obstinacy until, at breakfast, on the day Granny had in mind to make her trip Ginga would announce, not always with good grace, that he could spare a couple of hours – but no more – to take her. As, due to the slowness of the speed at which he drove, the twelve-mile journey could take anything between thirty minutes and three-quarters of an hour in each direction, this meant that Granny, upon arriving in town, was forced to do a round of the shops as if pursued by a swarm of bees before her allotted two hours expired.

While Granny changed her clothes and got herself ready, collecting shopping bags and lists and seeing to it that I was in a fit state to go to town with her, Ginga was out in the garage, pipe billowing clouds of smoke, trying to start the engine of the car. When cold, this always had to be done manually and involved a series of rapid turnings of a long handle inserted in the engine in order to crank it into life. The Hillman was a temperamental little car. More often than not the engine refused to start, beyond making a few uncertain wheezes and splutters before dying with a resounding gasp. From the house, Granny and I would hear Ginga swearing as his efforts were thwarted and the sound of cranking became more frenzied – and useless. Almost as soon as she had whispered to me, a smile around her lips, to run along and help him, a bellow would come from outdoors,

'Send out the boy.'

Out I would run, along the garden path, past the onion-scented chives, the massed ranks of potatoes, the hollyhocks, the fruit bushes drooping beneath the weight of their berries. Red-faced and dripping with perspiration, Ginga would order me into the car with instructions to depress the accelerator, in order to hasten the firing of the reluctant engine, as he cranked the starting handle. Once in the driving seat, foot pressing the pedal, I peered down the long, narrow bonnet of the car, past the large temperature gauge mounted on the radiator, and waited for Ginga to bend down, partially out of sight, in order to swing the starting handle. With the accelerator pedal down, flat on the floorboards, the engine normally fired straight away. But I was not to have my pleasure curtailed in such an arbitrary fashion. Quickly, before Ginga could straighten up, I turned off the ignition switch. The engine, which had been gathering strength in a promising fashion, faltered; then died.

'Did you take your foot off the throttle?' he shouted in dismayed disbelief.

'No, Ginga,' I replied, smiling righteously.

'Damn me – what's the matter with this bloody car?' would come the inevitable reply.

The catches fastening the leaves of the bonnet were snapped open and he peered inside, poking and prodding, scratching his head, relighting his pipe while he pondered the problem. Of course, by this time I had returned the ignition switch to the 'on' position, so was able to sit in safety while awaiting fresh developments. After a couple of minutes down slammed the bonnet leaves.

'We'll have another go. And be sure to keep your foot on that pedal.'

'Okay, Ginga, just as you say. Whenever you're ready.'

I normally repeated my trick a few more times until Ginga, goaded now to the point of complete frustration and seething rage, announced himself ready to abandon the journey.

'Oh, no,' I called, disappointment written clearly on my features. 'Please, Ginga. Just once more.'

'All right then. But just once, mind.'

This time I allowed the engine to fire without interruption

and showed my enthusiasm by revving it with furious pressings of the accelerator, which sent black smoke belching from the exhaust and caused Granny to arrive, breathless, from the house, clutching shopping baskets and a bag of sweets for the journey. She was anxious to be away from the place and heading towards Nairn in case Ginga, by now in a state of angry exhaustion, suddenly changed his mind and refused to budge. It had been known to happen – on more than one occasion.

Like all good games it had to end sometime. One day Ginga caught me in the act of turning off the ignition switch. He laughed at my trick, but said nothing. Later, while out in the woods visiting his pheasant coverts, he told me to make myself comfortable on a huge mound under a pine tree in order to eat my sandwiches and drink my flask of tea. He would be back in a few minutes, he said. I sank down into the soft mound and prepared to enjoy my feast. Within seconds hundreds of large, black ants were crawling over my body – up my legs, down my arms, across my neck, into my hair, inside my shirt – biting and nipping furiously, angered by my disturbance of their nest. When Ginga returned, from where, no doubt, he had watched his revenge unfolding from behind a tree, I was leaping about smacking and beating at the scurrying ants. He expressed astonishment, even sympathy, for my plight. But I knew I had been duped. I could see the twinkle in his eyes as he tried to suppress a grin; just as, on many occasions, I too had bottled up my laughter and looked innocent when he swung the starting handle of an engine rendered dead by my own treacherous hand.

So, off we would go along the narrow road, smoke pouring from the exhaust, more smoke streaming through the open window from Ginga's pipe. Once grinding along, often in second gear, occasionally in top, Ginga would start to relax, staring at the passing fields and woods for signs of vermin with a gamekeeper's keen and practised eye. It was also a time for the study of numbers of game birds. If a satisfying covey of pheasants or partridges was spotted, strutting around in a field, Ginga's instinctive reaction was to count them with no thought of the road ahead. Off we would veer to the right while he counted aloud and raised himself up in his seat for a better view. With the Hillman now on the wrong side of the road, ready to mount the opposite verge, control would be established by Granny grabbing at the steering wheel and wrenching the car back on course. This necessary action always brought shouts of protest from Ginga about her interfering with his driving and how such hasty behaviour could very well result in a nasty accident.

Granny maintained a tight-lipped silence throughout it all. However, there was one spot where she usually exclaimed in alarm. A junction, near a bend on a major road, should have meant Ginga stopping to watch for oncoming traffic. But the junction was on a hill. Because of his problems with gears on hills he never stopped, but always sailed out like a bird to join the main road. Poor Granny never failed to yell at this point. Her side of the car was nearest to the bend. Ginga, relieved to be out on the main road unscathed, silenced her by maintaining he'd always handled that junction in such a way and would go on doing so, despite what she said or how she behaved. He did; for several more years. Then he crashed into a car which, having priority, rounded the bend at speed to be confronted by the little Hillman crossing its path.

In court a few weeks later, Ginga told the magistrate that the accident was the other driver's fault. He was speeding, protested my irate grandfather. Going far too fast for safety. And furthermore, added Ginga, he had used that junction for twenty-five years and more and never been hit once by oncoming traffic until, as he put it a trifle undiplomatically, pointing an accusing finger at the amazed motorist sitting in the public benches in the courtroom,

'That bloody fool came winging round the bend like a bat out of hell.'

Ginga was fined five pounds for careless driving. Enraged by this injustice, he drove away from the courthouse in a foul temper. As Granny remonstrated with him, urging calmness and reason, he emerged from a side street and ploughed into the side of a passing bus. A considerable commotion ensued, the least of which was the fact that both vehicles were slewed around at awkward angles, thus blocking the narrow street for some time.

Two weeks later he was fined a further five pounds after failing to convince an incredulous magistrate (the same one as before) that this time it was the bus driver's fault. From then on Granny's journeys by car became fewer: only to be undertaken when absolutely necessary. And when they were, she sat beside her husband and prayed in silence that both would return from the shopping expedition without being maimed or even killed; and that Ginga would not be forced yet again to run the gauntlet of Scottish justice, a subject which he now discussed ad nauseam and which he viewed with a jaundiced and distinctly disparaging eye.

8

Topping the bill at many of the concerts held in the hall over the years was 'The Singing Molecatcher'. A small, sprightly man with black hair and black, bushy eyebrows, he sang songs – both happy and sad – about the vagaries of farm life and thwarted love; and of heather-clad hills and desolate glens with tumbledown cottages in which mothers wept for their sons and daughters now emigrated far away to Australia, Canada, New Zealand or the United States of America. And all the while, as he sang, he walked about the stage accompanying his ditties on a button-key melodeon, jet black with a mother-of-pearl facing, which caught the reflection from the footlights to radiate sparkling, twinkling arcs of lights like flashing stars into the uplifted eyes of the audience.

He always finished his act with a medley of Scottish country dance tunes, ending with a fast foot-stomping reel. This brought the audience to its feet, cheering and whistling, until the perspiring molecatcher, wiping his face and forehead with a large, red polka-dot handkerchief, agreed to return to provide an encore. And when this was over, never once, sometimes twice, more usually for the third or fourth time, 'The Singing Molecatcher' would bring the rest of the concert party on to the stage to acknowledge the rapturous applause. Together, artistes and audience would then raise the roof with the National Anthem, melodeon, piano, violin and occasionally a musical saw providing the music to which we all gave of our best and sang.

Invariably, with the concert over, the chairs would be stacked away in a back room, or spread around the sides of the hall and the floor cleared, ready for the dance. Meanwhile, those in the audience who were staying for further late-night revels drank tea and ate sandwiches and cakes and discussed the merits of the first part of the evening's entertainment.

'The Singing Molecatcher' – who, when he wasn't performing in country halls throughout the Highlands and north-east of Scotland, actually went from farm to farm in a tiny van attempting to halt the ravages of the burrowing mole population – was a great favourite with young and old. To have his concert party in the hall guaranteed the organisers of the function – the badminton club, the drama society, the indoor bowling group, the Women's Rural Institute branch – a handsome profit from the sale of tickets. There were some, however, usually the very elderly, who had attended concerts for more years than anyone – even themselves – could remember, who thought that he repeated the same old programme night after night.

'He's been singing yon song for years,' they would say; or, 'You'd have thought he'd have learned a few more tunes to play on his wee boxie after a' this time,' you would hear them muttering to each other as the applause died down.

All the same, detractors and fans alike flocked to the hall whenever the posters, attached to roadside trees and telegraph poles, went up to announce an impending visit. And good though the other acts might be – the comedian with his songs and patter; the young, kilted piano-accordion player who dazzled the audience with an amazing display of pyrotechnics on the keyboard; the matronly soprano with her renditions of the love songs of Robert Burns; the man with the musical saw, whose whining, whistling, eerie tones produced from a violently bent saw blade, played with a violin bow, set many teeth on edge and ears buzzing painfully – it was the act at the top of the bill which everyone had come to see and hear.

So, after the interval there was a shiver of anticipatory pleasure in the air when the master of ceremonies strode on to the stage to announce,

'It's the moment you've all been waiting for. So, ladies and gentlemen, a hefty round of applause – please! Clap hands, one and all, for – The Singing Molecatcher!'

And out from the wings and on to the platform he would bound, smiling and dancing a little jig, his fingers roaming nimbly over the melodeon's buttons without so much as a downwards glance, the first of his songs already bursting forth to delight row upon row of expectant faces, necks craning for a better view, hard seats forgotten, while for forty-five minutes or more he would hold us all in his skilfully woven spell. Even the clink of the crockery in the kitchen was silenced and the hissing, bubbling, steam-erupting belching of the tea urn muted to acceptable levels while he was on stage. Outside, a gale could be howling, rain or sleet could be pounding against the windows, but in the warm, smoke-filled, steam-dampened hall, everything – good news and bad – was forgotten while the soft, lilting cadences of the molecatcher's voice and the sonorous tones of his melodeon drowned all the other sounds to unite a community in pleasure and in joy.

In addition to the visiting concert parties, headed by semi-professionals such as the molecatcher, amateur concerts took place from time to time. There were plenty of people in the district who could sing a few songs, play the violin, the accordion or the bagpipes, and any organiser had little difficulty in putting together a show comprised of local talent, both good and bad. These, too, were well attended because of the opportunities on various levels for enjoying oneself; to either appreciate something well done by someone you knew or to relish the awfulness of the badly done and view with hilarity the discomfort of the not-so-well-loved local figure forgetting the lines of a poem or faltering midway through a song when either minds went blank or accompanying pianists transposed the music in too high a key for the singer to cope.

My mother had a good singing voice and was usually available to give a rendering of 'My Alice Blue Gown' which, no matter how many times she sang it, seemed to delight each new audience. As the piano accompanist for these impromptu local concerts was Miss Milne, the schoolteacher, it was not long before I was being pressed into service. I enjoyed my singing appearances, revelling in the cheers and applause for my efforts. 'Down in the Glen', 'The Garden Where the Praties Grow', 'Westering Home', and 'The Road to the Isles' were in my standard repertoire. Also included for light comic relief were two songs made famous by Sir Harry Lauder, 'Roamin' in the Gloamin'' and 'Keep Right On to the End of the Road' which I sang enthusiastically while striding around the stage brandishing a crooked walking stick in a wild impersonation of the renowned entertainer.

However, my *pièce de résistance* was the song I had sung to the teacher on my first day in school, 'The Muckin' o' Geordie's Byre'. Even someone of my tender years was shrewd enough to realise that this was the song best suited to bringing my selection to a rousing finish. Because it was a song about farming life many in the audience were familiar with the scenes described in its innumerable verses; and I unashamedly played to the gallery by miming activities such as milking a cow and shovelling muck while, supposedly, suffering from a bout of heavy drinking. Getting the audience to take part in the singing of the chorus was my final piece of uninhibited, extravagant showmanship. While I sang even louder Miss Milne perspired and dust rose in clouds from the quivering piano as she played fortissimo, one eye on the sheet of music, the other on my prancing figure striding about the stage goading, with feverish arm-waving, the audience to fresh heights of participation.

There was one occasion when Miss Milne had the bright idea of my singing a duet with a girl a year or so older than me.

Valerie, the sister of James, the hymn-singing farmer's son, was an attractive and high-spirited ten-year-old. For some reason best known only to herself Miss Milne chose as our song a sentimental and romantic Victorian ballad entitled 'The Keys of Heaven'.

The embarrassment caused to us both was a delight to the other occupants of the classroom as day after day prior to the concert we were cajoled and prodded through the series of coy and flirtatious verses. Not only was I required to sing such lines as 'I will give you the key to my heart' and 'Madam, will you walk and talk with me?' but had to act the role of a determined and sincere lover intent on winning the affection and hand in marriage of a fair, young maiden. Valerie, although prone to giggling and a certain amount of blushing, seemed to take the duet a little more seriously than I did, clutching me to her with imprisoning arms when the moment came for her to signify acceptance of my oft-repeated declarations of love. With muffled sniggering and muted wolf-whistles the other boys watched Miss Milne make me go down on bended knee on the dusty floor alongside the piano and look imploringly into Valerie's eyes as I beseeched her to marry me. And Valerie, taller and more broad-shouldered than I ever would be, looked down on her grovelling lover and smirked, acting for all her worth the part of the woman playing hard to get. Of course, as this was a daily spectacle the classroom viewed the rehearsals with mounting excitement and glee as each day passed. On several occasions Miss Milne was forced to temporarily abandon the proceedings and berate the onlookers, exhorting them to 'be your age' and as a punishment issuing more work to keep them occupied until, once more, she could give them her full attention.

When the evening of the concert arrived we were both word perfect; and knew exactly what to do. In order to lend authority to the Victorian setting Valerie and I were in period costume.

She wore a gown of blue velvet which had been reconstructed from one of her grandmother's old dresses, with a lacy bonnet on her head tied under her chin by a delightful pink bow. This held my eyes in mesmerised fascination each time I gazed at it. It was agreed – even by me – that she looked very fetching.

My suit had been made after hours of painstaking and diligent labour by my mother and was red above and blue below. It could well have been a coveted and colourful possession in the wardrobe of Little Lord Fauntleroy. The only drawback was that the jacket and knickerbocker trousers were made with crêpe paper which rustled and whispered with every movement I made. Because of the limited elasticity of the crêpe it was extremely difficult to put on; and once encased within its creaking folds I could only lift my arms with a mechanical movement like that of a clockwork toy. To walk was like seeing a marionette suddenly come to life in a series of jerky, hesitant steps. All the same, like Valerie's gown, my suit was admired. People said I looked handsome. The kind words were lost on me. I merely felt like a fool; and was sure I looked like one.

On stage Valerie and I plodded on through our song, Miss Milne smiling now and then over her shoulder in a benevolent and kindly way at her two prancing prodigies. Valerie simpered in front of her ardent admirer while she held the hem of her gown between thumb and forefinger and curtseyed with what was supposed to be a mixture of respect and tantalising guile. I swayed this way and that, my cheeks blushing furiously, my body flushed with the sweat of embarrassed fear, now cold, now hot, the noise of my paper suit seeming to drown the thumping of my heart and the words of ardent love pouring from my trembling lips.

The climax of the song arrived when I had to throw myself on one knee and implore the fair young maid once and for all to agree to marry me. I had been instructed to raise my arms towards Valerie and extend my hands, palms upwards, as I knelt in front of her. And this I did, with a superb gesture, in a burst of excitement, the more to get it over with quickly than from any display of talented acting ability. At once my paper suit split beneath the arms and across my bottom. In an instant I was reduced from a strutting dandy to a ragged urchin. Horrified, I jumped up, clutching at the tattered remnants, knocking Valerie backwards and into Miss Milne who momentarily lost her way on the keyboard. There were some titters from the audience; a whispered 'Get on with it' from our disconcerted accompanist now searching with fumbling fingers for the correct keys; a black look from Valerie whose pretty bonnet had been knocked askew and was now at a rakish, jaunty angle over one ear and one eye. Then we were soaring through the final verse, Valerie now signifying she would be mine by throwing her arms around me, helping without knowing it to hold my ragged suit together, propelling me backwards into the centre of the stage. And there upon the crash of the final chords from the piano she sealed her promise with a resounding kiss as we clung together in a shambolic embrace amid a wave of applause.

When we left the stage Valerie laughed aloud at my tattered and dishevelled appearance. I burst into tears. Miss Milne murmured sympathetic words and my mother dried my eyes. It was to be my one and only appearance in a duet. And never again would I consent to the wearing of a crêpe paper suit.

9

I fell in love with Catriona when I was ten years old. She was twenty. She lived with her brother, Colin, in a small cottage surrounded by trees and a huddle of tumbledown sheds, home to a collection of motor cycles, both ancient and modern, and scores of hens, chickens, ducks and cats. Their scratching, clucking, egg laying, quacking and mewing spilled over into the yard, reducing it to a feather- and flea-infested dust-bowl in summer and a seeping quagmire of dropping-strewn mud throughout the long months of winter.

Catriona and Colin looked like twins, but Colin was actually several years older. Their lifestyle intrigued me because of the absence of parents or, seemingly, any other relatives. I never asked what had happened to their mother and father; and was never enlightened. Theirs was a happy, crazy, devil-may-care household, always full of laughter and high spirits due to the constant stream of visitors. These were either youngsters like myself or young men, mostly workers on local farms, eager to learn how to ride a motor cycle or master the complexity of the noisy, thumping, thudding engines.

Colin was an expert in all things mechanical, but motor cycles were his speciality. A farm worker by day, driving a tractor, ploughing the fields, bringing in the cows for milking, repairing the boundary fences, in the evenings he became a man transformed by his passion for motor cycles. With a shock of unruly hair, the colour of fine straw, and a perpetual grin on his grease-smeared, oil-blotched friendly face, he held court in his sheds, dispensing advice to all those who spluttered up the hill on faltering machines. There was always a motor cycle being rebuilt or repaired; Triumph, BSA, Matchless, Norton. At the rear of the sheds clumps of nettles and purple willow herb hid the rusting, cannibalised frames, engines and wheels of those machines which had been sacrificed in order that others could live again.

And when for one evening he had had enough of carburettors and chains, pistons and plugs, Colin would throw down his spanners and into the cottage we'd troop. After scrubbing the muck from his hands and arms, but more often than not still with a blackened face, he would reach for his other great love – a piano accordion. Although his fingers were stubby, the nails chipped and grimy, they roamed nimbly over the keyboard producing a magical cascade of tunes from the poignant romance of Italian love songs to the stirring bravura of 'Scotland the Brave'. Sometimes, when the tunes were of songs we knew, such as 'The Road to the Isles' or 'Westering Home' we would all join in, raising our chipped cups containing tea the colour of treacle or, if older, medicine glasses full to the brim with whisky produced by Catriona from a cupboard alongside the black, smoke-encrusted range. Cats of all shapes and sizes, coloured ginger, tabby and black, entered and left the kitchen throughout the singsong; and there was always a mother nursing kittens – or about to give birth to a litter – ensconced in a cardboard box beside the smoking fire.

Catriona was beautiful. Even in the cottage with its drab curtains hanging limply against fly-smeared windows, its furniture collected from a dozen different sales, the armchairs sagging, the table with two legs ravaged to half their normal width by clawing cats, she bloomed like a rare and exotic flower. Blonde like her brother, but taller, she had long, strong legs, a bust like a Hollywood film star and a face that smiled 'Welcome' to all who climbed the hill, scattering the hens and ducks, on the way to the porch with its canopy of writhing, overgrown, sweet-scented roses. Like Cinderella, she cooked the meals, cleaned the cottage, fed the cats, the hens and the ducks, clad in her oldest clothes; but on Friday evenings, when dances were either held in the local hall or somewhere in the surrounding district, Catriona was transformed into glittering elegance. Nylon stockings rustling, freshly ironed frock clinging to sculpted curves, she tiptoed regally through the mud to Colin's waiting motor cycle where, arms clutched tightly around his waist, she was spirited away to the bright lights, the smoke, the steam from the sputtering tea urns and the music which promised romance albeit for a few, brief midnight hours.

Such was her personality and general air of vivacity, together with startling good looks, that her admirers were many – and varied. They ranged across the spectrum of age; the wide-eyed devotion of ten-year-olds such as me who, with aching arms, would carry her shopping bags the two miles or so from the shop, while trying to keep pace with her rangy, long-legged stride, all for a smile and a ruffled head of hair; the youths and young men with longing in their eyes and in the suggestive posture of their bodies astride motor cycles trying to impress or cavorting playfully around her in the dusty yard; the older men, married for an age to their womenfolk, who waved from the fields as she went past, looked long and hard at her retreating figure, then sighed and went back to work – to dream.

Intuition must have made Catriona fully aware of her overwhelming popularity. Yet she showed no outward signs of using it to advantage. She remained sensible, hard working (she did spells of seasonal work on various farms, especially at harvest-time and when the potato crop was ready for lifting), quiet and unassuming. But when it came to Friday evenings and dance nights she emerged from the cottage like the goddess she was to dazzle and charm all who pursued her through foxtrot and quickstep, military two-step and old-time waltz. Her popularity in the hall enraged and infuriated some of her less charitable female contemporaries, but most were content to watch with no more than a deep, wistful sigh of envy and the wish that they, too, had the same appeal; the sort of allure which brought men, some of whom had never danced in their lives, bounding in her direction to sweep her into their arms and on to the floor.

The dances were great social occasions. Most took place directly after some other event, a concert, whist drive, a play performed by the amateur dramatic club or, occasionally, a badminton tournament. The result of this was a hall full of people of every age, from grandsons and granddaughters to grandfathers and grandmothers, many of whom had been present at the earlier event, had stayed for the tea, sandwiches and cakes and were determined to make a night of it by attending the dance as well.

The two local newspapers in Forres, the *Gazette* and the *News* (which everyone referred to as the *Squeak* because of its outspoken pronouncements on local affairs), carried many advertisements every week for Friday evening entertainment all over the county and, in particular, in the districts surrounding the town. Usually, if a concert or a whist drive preceded a dance, it would be stated in bold type, *Dancing to Commence at 10.30 p.m.* By then there would normally be a crowd standing outside the hall door waiting for admittance; local men and girls who had come by bicycle, motor cycle and car, or on foot, and those from further afield in one, sometimes two, specially hired coaches.

No alcohol was sold in the hall – only soft drinks – and neither was any supposed to be consumed on the premises. A faded, greasy, tattered notice proclaimed this warning, while hinting at dire penalties, on the door of the men's cloakroom. However, this in no way deterred the consumption of whisky and beer in the surrounding wood and in the car park; and when the time came for the doors to open, many of the men who surged forward in the throng had drunk enough to give them a feeling of either argumentative bravado or expansive bonhomie. However, most of the sensible ones had judged their intake to such a degree that they stayed out of the clutches of the stewards (usually two burly farmers) whose job it was to watch for potential troublemakers and refuse them entry. Of course, when a proper drunk was apprehended trying to push his way through was the moment any trouble usually erupted; sometimes a fist fight, but more often a rapid burst of shouting, swearing and shoving by both sides, ending with the drunk staggering off into the darkness yelling threats of a blood-curdling nature against the victorious doorkeepers and anyone even remotely associated with them.

As the band set up their music and instruments on the stage and the newcomers sorted themselves out around the hall it was time for the tea-drinking men to down their cups and push against the tide to reach the open air. Knowing nods and winks were exchanged between friends as little groups converged at the foot of the steps, then began to congregate beneath the windows from which narrow beams of light lanced the blackness of the night. There they released from bulging jacket pockets imprisoned half-bottles of whisky or dragged from some secret lair in the brambles and bracken paper carrier bags of clinking, rattling bottles of beer. These were passed around from mouth to mouth, their contents gulped at and savoured as if in some deadly oath-taking ritual, while after a crashing drum roll from within the strains of saxophone and accordion sang out and the first waltz of the evening got off to an awkward, hesitant, uncertain start.

The programme of dances was divided in fairly equal proportions between Scottish country dances and traditional favourites such as the Eightsome Reel, the Dashing White

Sergeant, the Valetta and the Military Two-Step, and modern, ranging from the Quickstep and Slow Foxtrot through to the more daring Rumba, Samba or Tango. In this way the band provided entertainment for all ages, both on the floor and grouped on the benches placed along the walls and beneath the stage.

In the main, with the exception of a handful of couples who couldn't bear to let their respective partners out of their sight, the women were ranged at one side, the men at the other. There was also usually a huddle of men close to the door, thus ensuring themselves of a speedy (and unobtrusive) exit whenever it was felt the time had arrived for another drinking session behind the hall. The area in front of the stage was normally occupied by those girls who fancied someone in the band or hard-of-hearing elderly matrons and men anxious to be close enough in order to hear the music. Such was the volume from the loudspeakers at either end of the platform it was hard to be anywhere near this area without being partially deaf; but on most occasions the prime seats were taken by the same old couples who shouted their gossip back and fore in ceaseless volleys as the saxophone wailed, the accordion droned and the drums beat out a tattoo only feet away from their grey-haired or balding, nodding heads.

The oldest of the old, whose dancing days were over, and the young, without knowledge of the proper steps, watched from the sidelines and revelled in their role of self-appointed voyeurs. Their interest in the behaviour of others was absolute and totally unashamed. Hiding something from the all-pervading scrutiny of their probing, prying eyes was well nigh impossible. It gave hours of constant pleasure to be a witness to the blossoming of romances, to see who had been left in the lurch, who was still on the shelf and, to the delight of the youngsters (most of whom knew more than ever showed on their innocent faces), and the disapproval of their elders, especially the women, which girls were deliberately flaunting themselves in the hope of finding a man, merely for the night.

Maggie was one such girl. When her father, an estate worker, committed suicide when she was twelve years old she was freed, at last, from the confines of rigid discipline. A foultempered, withdrawn man, he had ruled his family – wife and four children – with the traditional iron fist. His wife, a diminutive woman, lined and bent by submission and drudgery, was frequently to be seen with bruises and grazes, the result of yet another battle lost in an unending and one-sided struggle. He used a leather belt to beat the children and needed little provocation for an excuse to wield it. As a result the younger children – two boys and a girl – were like mice, peeping from hidden corners in house or garden when a visitor called. Only Maggie, black haired, full lipped and sultry, maintained an aura of pride and independence in the midst of this unhappy and repressive atmosphere. However, even she quailed in the presence of her brooding, brutal father.

One Sunday afternoon he hanged himself with a length of cable fastened to a massive bough on a pine tree overhanging a narrow gorge on a lonely, secluded part of the river. 'His head was almost severed from his shoulders' was a whispered remark which one boy heard pass between a tea-drinking policeman and his shocked but attentive mother. For days we talked about nothing else while at school. And for months that remark was to haunt my imagination both in my waking hours and in the depths of fevered, troubled sleep. Few mourned Maggie's father. It would have been difficult to find anyone who had ever had anything good to say about him when he was alive. So, Maggie and family were released from their bondage to a man they must have all despised, despite the indestructible ties of blood. Instead of their tied cottage they were given a small, tumbledown house in a remote corner of the estate on the fringe of open moorland. As a means of eking out a living the mother was able to do cleaning work at the Big House and seasonal work on some of the farms. The younger children started to emerge from the shadows, shyly and hesitantly; but for Maggie the new-found freedom was grasped without inhibition and, in a remarkably short space of time, with total abandon.

By the time she was fourteen she was attending dances in the hall on Friday evenings, lipstick shining, cheeks lightly rouged, hair styled and gleaming, a thin summer frock moulded to her ripening figure. On dance nights her bust appeared to be larger than usual, giving rise to the notion that she padded her bra especially for the occasion. Schoolboys of her own age, who claimed to have seen her without any clothes, said knowingly that she was really flat-chested. It always raised a laugh when someone would remark that Fat Donald, the roadman, had bigger breasts than the bold, pert Maggie.

But at the dances she ignored the sniggering youngsters, held her head aloof from the leering smiles and knowing winks, and went in search of more promising company. Like some frenetic butterfly she sought out the older youths and young men, in particular the farmers' sons who had cars. There was never a shortage of partners eager to be with her and as the dance progressed in the smoky, sweaty, dust-laden atmosphere of the hall, one by one she dispensed with her army of suitors. By one o'clock in the morning, when the band was wearily launching itself into the music for the last waltz, Maggie had chosen her mate and the winner wore an expression of excited triumph as they clung like limpets to each other's bodies while circling the floor. From the sidelines the rejected youths watched with expressions of envious lust, drooling over what might have been, cursing the lucky individual who would take her home via the back seat of his car, remarking loudly that 'that was the finish' as far as they were concerned between Maggie and themselves. But come the next dance they would all be there again, panting with eager anticipation, jockeying for position, as they lined up to dance with her, once more for yet another night of wild fantasies and delicious thoughts of what would surely be their prize luring them into her arms. Maggie played a shrewd and subtle game. Over, say, the space of a year, all the local admirers she really fancied had their turn. Spread a little happiness might well have been her motto. It was like a lottery – with prizes for all; in time.

The older women – and a few of the more prudish younger ones – viewed Maggie's antics with expressions bordering on horror. This was the very stuff of which scandals were made; and to a woman they were scandalised. This one or that one was always going to see to it that she spoke to Maggie's mother about her daughter's wayward conduct. It was agreed, quite emphatically, that someone had a duty to put a stop to it. Maggie's behaviour at the dances was shameless, quite shameless. The tongues wagged furiously. Gossip was rife. Why, after the last dance Mrs McDonald had actually seen Maggie's rusty bicycle being tied with rope across the open boot of young Jack Macarthur's car, then watched the pair of them kissing each other before belting off down the road in the direction of God knows where; to get up to God knows what for God knows how long? It was an absolute disgrace. The girl was being allowed to run wild. Someone would have to speak to Maggie's mother before the girl got herself into trouble.

The chosen someone was old Andrew Macintyre, a staunch elder of the church. He was considered to be the most God-fearing man in the district; the next best thing to the minister himself. And no-one wanted to bother the minister about such a delicate subject. The gossips were agreed on that point. Anyway, old Andrew was judged to be more pious and holy than any man of the cloth, with the advantage of having a forbidding nature and a sharp tongue when it came to making pronouncements of a moral nature. And had he not seen for himself, when he was cycling home from church one Sunday summer evening, Maggie and three or four boys bathing naked in a pool in the river? True, he hadn't actually seen them from the road. He had heard the laughter while pushing his bicycle up a hill and gone some distance into the wood in order to trace the source of the merriment. He'd had to part the bracken and push aside the hazel branches before obtaining a clear view of the river far below. The sight of the white, youthful bodies, naked as new-born babes, splashing and cavorting in the sun-dappled water, had quite unnerved him, so he'd said, that he'd felt quite faint. The sight still haunted him, so he said. It was not something he could easily forget. So, eventually, armed with this first-hand experience, Andrew Macintyre was despatched to Maggie's mother in the hope that his presence, with its strong aura of gloom, doom and damnation, would make her see the error of her ways regarding her wanton daughter.

She was out on the one and only evening he called at the house. Afterwards, all he would ever say about the visit was that only the eldest daughter was at home and there on the doorstep he'd spoken sharply and firmly to her about the shameless exhibition she was making of herself. It was, he considered, a much better outcome than having raised the matter with the mother. But when pressed for greater detail about his conversation and Maggie's reaction old Andrew always became evasive and was quick to change the subject. On the one hand people felt he was deliberately hiding something; but on the other hand he was Andrew Macintyre, pillar of the church. Yet, could it just be possible . . . ?

The truth, according to Maggie, who took immense delight in relating the story to every boy granted the freedom of her body, was that she'd been alone in the house, looking out from an upstairs window, when she'd seen 'Holy Willie' (as she referred to him) coming across the field towards the door. Idle bits of overheard adult conversations had been passed to her by several of her boyfriends so she had some idea of old Andrew's mission. Slipping off her frock and pants, she had gone downstairs and waited in the kitchen close to the window. Andrew knocked several times on the door and not content with getting no reply decided to check that, indeed, no-one was at home. She heard his boots on the path, then a shadow filled the window in front of the sink. He was craning forward, shading his eyes, pressing his round, red face against the glass, eyes searching the room. It was then that she'd danced across the floor and stood, legs spread and arms flung wide, only a few feet away from the prying gaze of God's right-hand man. For a moment he'd stared, rooted to the spot, eyes wide ('Like a rabbit caught by a weasel,' she told me), then blinking rapidly as if not believing what he was seeing. In an instant Maggie spun around, bent over to touch her toes, then having bared her bottom was facing the front once again; this time pressing her face against the glass, smiling and laughing and shouting,

'Come in. Come in. I'm here all on my own.'

It was all too much for old Andrew. He staggered backwards, an expression of having witnessed a ghost frozen on his features, to fall head over heels in the middle of some blackcurrant bushes. But wasting no time, he scrambled free and was away across the field as if a swarm of hornets was trying to settle on his head. From upstairs Maggie watched him mounting his bicycle to go wobbling off down the hill, almost colliding with some sheep sunning themselves in the middle of the grassy track.

She told me later – three years later, in fact, when she was seventeen and I was fourteen – that she had never laughed so much before – or since – at the sight of 'Holy Willie's' amazed, incredulous expression and at his mad, panic-stricken flight to escape the vision of nakedness presented in all its glory to his prying, censorius gaze. She would go on remembering it for ever, she said; and whenever she felt low in spirits and had had enough of life she'd think of it again and laugh, just like the first time, until her sides were sore and her throat ached.

To the surprise of those with faith in old Andrew's powers of persuasion, who could never envisage he would tell half a lie, let alone embroider a complete fabrication of the truth, Maggie's attendance at the Friday night dances was assured for years to come. It would be a couple of years or more before I would be pursuing her around the hall, attempting a portrayal of youthful sophistication while tripping and stumbling through Quickstep, Foxtrot, and Old-time Waltz. Meanwhile, apart from dancing sedate polkas and mannered waltzes with the mothers of my schoolfriends or girls of my own age, like Valerie, whose embarrassment and awkwardness at holding hands in public matched my own, I had to remain on the sidelines. Here, while listening to the music and eavesdropping on the gossip, I watched with rapture the vision of Catriona, elegant and beautiful, floating effortlessly in the arms of her partner; and wished with a passion akin to pain that I, too, was twenty years old and taking his place.

It was a dream; a fevered, romantic fantasy, exquisite in its intensity; a powerful torrent of emotion directed towards a distant point in time when the unattainable would, eventually, become mine. It was love, pure and simple, fired by something intangible; innocent adoration of beauty and charm, the more painful because the object of its focus was always within reach, yet might have been a million miles away. I think, in reality, I saw her as the ideal elder sister, the sister I never had, but who I imagined in my dreams was like all elder sisters to everyone; loving and caring while cloaked in a rare beauty that came from within to warm her smile and bring a special quality to her laughter.

I was never to dance with Catriona. By the age of twenty-two she was dead; one more victim to the scourge of tuberculosis which, like polio, was the dreaded disease of my childhood years.

Although I knew she was in hospital I had no comprehension that I would never see her again. When I heard the news I felt an ache and a pain so intense I could scarcely breathe. My hands shook and my legs turned to rubber, trembling violently when I made my way to the banks of the river to slump down on a grassy knoll above a rumbling waterfall. I lay with my head on my arms, weeping bitterly for the friend I had lost. The noise of the river masked the sound of my sobbing, but nothing could hide the depths of my grief. The salt from my tears tasted bitter in my mouth. It was a mark of the bitterness that would stay locked within me for some time to come.

And forever after, although I still went to see Colin and joined in the fun with motor cycles, accordion and songs, Catriona's cottage was a hollow shell now that her laughter had been silenced and her smile was no longer with us; a smile that had radiated kindness and love; the purest, most simple smile that was, to me, the finest and most enduring smile of all.

10

Who would true valour see,
Let him come hither;
One here will constant be,
Come wind, come weather;
There's no discouragement
Shall make him once relent
His first avowed intent
To be a pilgrim.

As the voices of the congregation in the church swirled upwards echoing across the length and breadth of the high ceiling and the organ prepared, with sonorous, dramatic chords, the way for the singing of the second verse, the bag of Imperial Mints came towards me, passed slowly from one hand to the next along the pew. It seemed to be taking an age to reach me as eager fingers fumbled and rummaged before being withdrawn to surreptitiously clutch the coveted pandrop against the cover of the open hymn book. There it would lie concealed until the singing of the hymn was over. The sermon came next. It might be fifteen minutes long; it might be thirty. Very occasionally, if the flock was in need of a forceful message they were required to remember, it was even longer. Only the minister knew. So, while he preached the faithful could console themselves by sucking on the mint, safe in the knowledge that a giant pandrop had the power to outlast any sermon yet devised. Somehow it was a comfort and made the minister's message easier to take.

Whoso beset him round,
With dismal stories:
Do but themselves confound,
His strength the more is;
No lion can him fright
He'll with a giant fight
But he will have a right
To be a pilgrim.

The paper bag drew nearer. Surely it would reach me before the end of the third and final verse. It was an unwritten rule, a tradition, that the pandrops must be removed from the bag *during* the singing of the hymn which preceded the sermon. Once it was over, rather like a version of musical chairs, the bag remained with the person in whose possession it was when the last notes rang out. But the rules of etiquette demanded that the contents must now remain inside the bag. In this way all the noise of rustling paper, the occasional sweet dropped by clumsy fingers to go rolling and bouncing along the floor, was obliterated by the voices and the powerful blast of the organ. Naturally, I was always on tenterhooks that somehow it might never reach me. As a result I sang the words of the hymn with one eye on the page of the hymn book and the other following the rate of progress of the sweets in my direction.

The bag of pandrops belonged to the station master who sat with his wife and daughter in the pew directly in front of my mother and me. He always provided the sweets, although when my mother went to church she usually took a few with her just in case the benefactor did not attend on that particular Sunday. It was always Imperial Mints; never toffees. One or two of the congregation did bring toffees with them. But you couldn't sing hymns holding a hymn book in both hands and unwrap a toffee at the same time. And if you waited and tried to get the paper off during the sermon the noise was enough to make heads turn to send disapproving glances in your direction.

There was one awful occasion when even the minister, high in his pulpit against the wall, heard the distinctive sound of a Sharp's toffee being slowly and furtively disrobed and had paused in mid-sentence to fix the offender with a distinctly unchristian, baleful eye.

One of the two elderly spinster sisters who sat next to my mother now had the bag. I glanced along at her. She seemed to be trying to decide whether or not to have a pandrop this morning. I silently urged her to hurry and make up her mind.

> Hobgoblin nor foul fiend
> Can daunt his spirit;
> He knows he at the end
> Shall life inherit;
> Then fancies fly away
> He'll fear not what men say
> He'll labour night and day
> To be a pilgrim.

The bag had arrived. Because of my age I was allowed two sweets. I withdrew them hastily during the prolonged 'Amen'. As the congregation coughed and spluttered and rearranged themselves once more on the hard pews I tapped the station master's shoulder and handed back the bag. He turned his head, smiled, pulled out a pandrop for himself, popped it into his mouth, then turned back to face the front in order to hear the words of wisdom. A large bulge in the side of his cheek marked the extent of his satisfaction.

Before the minister went aloft to the pulpit the church officer, known as the beadle, climbed the winding staircase carrying a Bible of enormous size and weight and arranged it on a lectern. He then descended, disappeared through a doorway leading to the vestry to return, seconds later, with a glass brimful of water. Making the ascent once again he placed the glass on a shelf at the front of the pulpit alongside the lectern. I was certain that one day, when the minister was waving his arms around while putting emphasis on some salient point in his sermon, he would knock the glass and send it toppling down and on to the organist's head. He never did. But I secretly hoped that he would – next time. This done, the beadle stood to one side and the minister climbed the steps. Once he was safely in the pulpit the beadle closed the door and hurried down to return to his pew.

The minister stood for a time either arranging the pages of his notes for the sermon or tugging at the folds of his black robes. After taking a sip from the glass of water he leaned forward, resting his hands on the sides of the lectern. His eyes roamed around the church as if taking stock of the mood of his congregation. Actually, I believed implicitly he was counting the number of heads in order to assess the attendance. I had always done my own head count by this time and longed to shout out the number to see if it tallied with his estimate. On one occasion I mentioned this wild idea to my mother. She was horror-stricken.

'You'll do no such thing,' she admonished, giving me a thunderous glare. But a few seconds later, when she thought I wasn't looking, I'm sure I saw her smiling; quietly, just to herself.

The minister was not one of the firebrand school of preachers. Indeed, the Church of Scotland was not particularly noted for its messages of hell and damnation for all who failed to toe the spiritual line or strayed from the narrow path of righteousness. This was regarded as the preserve of the Free Church of Scotland and the Free Presbyterian Church, both of which bodies were regarded by some people as treading an extremely narrow and blinkered path in matters of doctrinal interpretation. Neither church had any foothold in our community. The Church of Scotland had us to itself.

Unlike the Free Churches where, it was said, the attendance records of parishioners were scrutinised in order to ensure strict adherence to the faith, people either attended our Sunday services – or they stayed away. And no questions were asked. Some, like my father, attended only once a year, clad in black overcoat and bowler hat reeking of mothballs, on Remembrance Sunday in November when a wreath-laying ceremony took place at the tiny war memorial. Others, including some farmers and many farm workers, made Harvest Thanksgiving Sunday their particular occasion to swell the numbers of the normally fairly small congregation.

In the church everyone had his or her own individual pew which, on those Sundays when the faithful were few, led to the incongruity of, say, Miss Milne, the schoolteacher, and her sister at one end with perhaps half the length of the building empty until the next place was occupied by old Andrew Macintyre, clad in black, summer and winter, tie knotted tightly in starched white collar, black boots gleaming like those of a private on parade. Other members of the congregation were similarly isolated in little pockets, both upstairs and down. At one end in the front of the gallery was a pew reserved for the laird and his family. Their appearances were few and far between, however, because their visits to the estate were limited to no more than several months in the year, spread over the month of August for the grouse shooting, Christmas and New Year and in the spring when the salmon fishing was at its best.

Going upstairs was considered rather a snobbish thing to do and only a few attempted it; even fewer persisted. One who did was a retired army man, a colonel of florid face and bristling moustache and highly checked Harris tweed suits smelling of a mixture of damp and tobacco smoke. One Sunday morning during the singing of Psalm 23 a cloud of smoke wafted out from around his neat figure in the pew next to the organ pipes. Suddenly, his wife shrieked, then strangled the cry by crushing a hand against her mouth. As one the pair rose in their seats, both beating frantically at the colonel's gaily checked jacket. The psalm continued, voices faltering slightly as heads turned and necks were craned in order to see better the commotion going on aloft. From his pulpit on the opposite wall the minister, raised to a level with the gallery, stared across in amazement as the frantic and, by now, almost hysterical pair danced a fair semblance of a jig around each other, before sprinting for the door leading to the stairs.

It was ten minutes or more before they reappeared, shoulders bowed, extremely chastened, entering on tiptoe to creep furtively towards their hastily vacated seats. The wife's face was white, the colonel's was redder than usual. And his jacket showed signs of severe charring and having been dowsed with water. A ragged, black patch covered the area where the side pocket had been. He was never again seen smoking his pipe before a church service; nor, for that matter, was it ever seen clenched firmly in his teeth as he was driven homewards after the service was over. On Sundays from then on the colonel's pipe stayed unlit and at home. Local opinion was unanimous that once again his wife, quite firmly, would see to that.

Harvest Thanksgiving was a wonderful time. On this occasion, as for the Remembrance Day service, the church was crowded. Both had a special significance for the community, the former because the lives and livelihoods of so many, young and old, were linked inexorably to the land; the latter due to the untimely death of too many local men fighting in both the First and Second World Wars, their names inscribed on a granite memorial stone set into the bank on a bend on the main road.

At Harvest Thanksgiving the church was alive with a rich and heady pot-pourri of tantalising smells. There was the dark loam clinging to the mounds of potatoes and turnips; the warm, dry comforting aroma of straw from the sheaves of oats and barley adorning the ends of the pews, the doorways and the front of the pulpit; the succulence of apples and plums, blackcurrants, redcurrants, gooseberries and raspberries in teeming baskets and bowls; the homely reminders of kitchens and warm ovens from the trestle tables bending beneath the weight of sponges, some filled with jam, others with butter icing, all jostling for pride of place alongside fruit cakes, large and small, shortbread, scones, oatcakes and loaves of bread of infinite shape and variety; a lingering hint of farmyard and hen-run from the baskets of eggs, white and brown, speckled and streaked, here and there a downy feather still clinging to the wiped and polished shells.

If the morning of the service was fine and dry and the sun shone strongly enough to remind everyone of the glories of the summer now past, shafts of light (sunbeams, as I called them) slanted in through the high, narrow windows to reflect amber and gold, scarlet and orange from row upon row of jars of bottled fruit and pots of jelly and jam and dark heather honey.

The entire display, mounted like some flamboyant exhibition along the aisles and in all corners of the church, highlighted every so often by bowls of sweet-scented roses and tall vases of dahlias, sweet peas and chrysanthemums, crimson and yellow, pink and bronze, was an act of thanks and praise, of homage and benevolence. The following day all the produce was taken to Forres to be distributed between the hospital and the old people's home.

So, when the organ played the opening bars of 'We Plough the Fields and Scatter' and in one mighty chorus, a trifle ragged at the edges, we sang of sowing 'the good seed on the land' the fruits of all our labours were there for everyone to see. And we were proud of them, no matter how minor a part some of us might have played in this annual cycle. And for the smaller members of the congregation, pandrop-sucking sprites such as me casting covetous glances at the tempting heaps of apples and plums, eyeing with longing the products of the kitchen, there was always the consolation of knowing that for every sponge dusted with icing sugar, every cake glistening with currants, within easy reach of where we sat, our mothers had baked a replica which sat safely at home awaiting our return.

Alongside the church and the graveyard was the Glebe Farm straddling the winding driveway up to the sprawling manse where the minister lived. Glebe farms were a feature of country churches, thus ensuring the manse of its own supply of milk, butter, cheese, eggs and, at appropriate times of the year, fresh chicken or turkey for the table. There were several fields, none of them very large, for the grazing of cattle and the growing of oats, potatoes and turnips; the corn going to the hens for food and the straw as bedding and feed, with the turnips, for the cows in their snug, stone-walled byre during the winter months. The potatoes were for the manse and farm kitchens, with any surplus being sold.

Old Andy was church beadle and tenant of Glebe Farm. With the aid of a rusting, whining, snorting, smoking Fordson tractor of formidable age and an assortment of decrepit implements he tilled the fields and harvested the crops; rattling backwards and forwards in all weathers, a tattered army greatcoat fastened around his body with a length of binder twine, as he rose up and down and heaved from side to side in an amazingly uncomfortable bucket seat. Running the farm was a secondary occupation for Andy, his main employment being as a horseman for a firm of timber contractors.

It was Andy's job to see to the dragging of felled trees from the most inaccessible regions of the forest, using two, and sometimes four, enormous cart horses. With chains and ropes Andy and his powerful horses hauled the fallen trees and lengths of sawn timber up and down the steepest of slopes, through rushing streams, over boulders and rocks, until they reached a woodland track. There, if the ground was firm enough to bear the weight of a lorry, the timber was stacked in great piles to await collection and transportation to the sawmill. More often than not the rain would have turned the trackway into an oozing ribbon of mud. If so, it was then up to Andy and his muscular, chestnut horses to get the wood by cart as far as the nearest road. It was hard, back-breaking work, a constant test of strength for man and beasts against the elements and the problems caused by the difficult and, at times, hostile terrain. But day after day, in winter storms and in summer heat, old Andy was there at work with his team of giants. Someone once told me,

'Yon horses will do anything for old Andy, because he treats them right. He's got a fine way with beasts, has yon man.'

It was perfectly true. By stroking their necks and talking incessantly to them as they laboured together, he achieved feats of strength and endurance from the horses that amazed anyone lucky enough to see them. The evidence spoke for itself; the trunks of mammoth pine, fir and spruce trees, shorn of their branches, the resin bleeding from myriad axe cuts, lying at the roadside having been hauled a mile or more across the sort of countryside which would have been considered too difficult for an army assault course.

And when Andy's long, exhausting day in the forest was over it was home to a meal, a pipe at the fireside, then out to work at one of a dozen different jobs on the farm. Old Andy never seemed to stop working. If not in the forest or out in the fields he could be seen at the church, up on the roof replacing slates, painting the guttering, repairing the bell tower; or somewhere in the graveyard mowing the grass, tidying the edges of the paths, sweeping fallen leaves, spending some time around the tombstones of graves no longer visited because, due to the passage of time, there was no-one left alive whose family duty it might be to visit them. And in the church itself on Sunday mornings, clad in black suit and stiff, white collar, he saw that all was in order for the service, from the laying-out of hymn books to filling the glass of water which would refresh the minister during the preaching of his sermon.

Mrs Andy was equally industrious. A hefty, florid-faced woman with greying hair knotted at the back in a tight bun, always covered by a net, she ran the farm during her husband's daily absences in the surrounding forests. She milked the cows and reared the calves, fed the hens and turkeys and collected the eggs, cleaned out the byre, shovelling and forking the old straw and muck into a huge, oozing, plopping, strong-smelling midden in the centre of the cobbled courtyard. In winter the surface was wet and slippery; in summer a crust formed, cracked and pitted like solidified lava. I was unfortunate enough to fall through the crust one day, having been dared to climb up and over the heap of muck. When I sank through the surface the smell was evil and the rotting dung reached my waist before I was able to haul myself out. Despite several hot baths (and a lecture from my mother about the general state of my intelligence – or lack of it) the smell lingered in my nostrils for days.

Mrs Andy also baked mouth-watering cakes and sponges, churned butter and made cheese; and when a hen's egg-laying days were over it was she who would catch the bird and wring its neck, before plucking it ready for the oven or the pot. Just as her husband kept a watchful eye on the exterior and surrounds of the church, it was Mrs Andy's job to clean, dust, scrub and polish the interior. And this she did with extraordinary dedication. The church reeked of the sweet scent of Mansion polish and the metallic tang of Brasso.

The uncarpeted flagstones were burnished by successive applications of Vim and hot water.

While old Andy was an amiable, placid individual, Mrs Andy was blunt and forthright. She said what she meant; and meant what she said. There were some who resented this attitude, mistaking it for rudeness; and youngsters, like myself, always approached her with a certain amount of trepidation, based on adult opinion and general gossip. All the same, if faced with politeness and an innocent smile her manner, although stern and brusque, was always kindly.

It was my job each day about half past six, after my evening meal, to cycle to old Andy's farm to collect our milk. Two gallons were required, to be shared between the household and my father's growing army of hard-working, hungry spaniels. For this I hung two metal milk pails, complete with lids, on either side of the handlebars of my bicycle. Every other day there was a third pail, lidless and much battered. This was needed to gather water from a spring which seeped through a dark and overgrown clump of bushes and trees to cascade over rocks down the bank at the side of the driveway. The water was essential for the survival of my goldfish, earlier examples of the species having proved by dying within forty-eight hours that the tap water, pure though its source might be, was incapable of sustaining life in a small, round bowl.

I was determined to keep fish number three alive. He had been won at a travelling fairground by skill and good luck (considering the barrel was bent) by my grandfather using an air rifle. On the way home the jam jar, with its tiny occupant, was knocked over in the rear of the car. At least five minutes elapsed before I was able to find the wriggling fish trapped in a fold in the carpet under my grandmother's seat. And a further sixty minutes or so went past before I reached home, with it gasping and thrashing in the minuscule amount of water still contained in the jar. Having survived this near-tragic chain of events I felt I owed the little fish some special treatment. I decided to experiment by using the water from the spring. It was an instant success. The fish lived for over six years, swimming happily in water the colour of weak tea containing traces of sediment and decaying vegetation. Its longevity was only achieved by regular replenishment of the contents of the bowl. Thus it was that every two days the journey homewards from old Andy's farm was even more dangerous than usual as I wobbled from side to side of the narrow road, two gallons of milk and one gallon of water slopping and sloshing inside the pails dangling from the handlebars. At times it was so hazardous and the weight of milk and water so unevenly distributed that accidents occurred, resulting in either grazed knees and elbows, or the loss of the milk, sometimes both.

As often as possible I tried to get to Glebe Farm when the milking of the cows was in progress. The byre, with its cobbled stone floor and wooden partitions dividing the stalls, was ripe with the intermingled smells of cow dung, dry, crackling straw and the warm, creamy milk foaming and frothing in the white enamel bucket clutched firmly between the milker's knees. Both Andy and his wife milked the four sturdy black and white cows, he with his cap turned round back to front so that he could press his head against the cow's side; she, hair net rigidly in place, lips in a thin, tight line, as with studied determination she squeezed the teats on the bulging udders and the milk flowed forth with a hiss and a squelch as it entered the bucket. The pair sat on small, hard three-legged stools, the kind favoured by pretty young milkmaids in children's illustrated storybooks; and occasionally, just as in the storybooks, there were accidents when, stool, occupants and milk bucket were knocked over by the sudden movement of a frustrated or nervous animal.

Three of the cows were docile, prepared even to suffer at my hands as Mrs Andy tried to teach me the rudiments of milking, but the fourth was a hulking, obstreperous lout of a cow with a mind of her own. Six evenings out of seven she was spoiling for trouble, jerking at the rope around her neck, lashing out with her hind legs, bellowing for all her worth so that the demented sound could be heard far from the farm to set up a chain reaction among other cattle until then grazing quietly and contentedly in neighbouring fields. Normally, it was old Andy's job to handle 'the wild one' as they both called her. There was constant talk of getting rid of her, but she was a good mother when it came to calf rearing and her milk yield was high; so, wild or not, she stayed on at Glebe Farm, tormenting her owners and threatening anyone foolish enough to enter a field in which she might be grazing.

She was as good as any bull when it came to a head-down, snorting charge. And to add extra menace to her appearance she possessed a spectacular pair of dangerously curved horns. Those of us who had seen pictures and read stories about bull fighters in Spain used to play a game on the way to and from school by clambering over the stone wall surrounding the field and waving our pullovers and handkerchiefs in her direction. She was always quick to respond. Tail high, head lowered, she would stampede in our direction while we scattered, shrieking and laughing, racing for the safety of the wall with the sound of her drumming hooves close behind. We always got away, usually because we never strayed too far into the field, although now and then as we grew more daring there were nasty moments when the wall seemed too far away, or we slipped while trying to get over it; and we waited for the lowered horns to go ripping into our backs as we squealed in terror and hauled ourselves up and over just in time.

There was once when Mrs Andy saw four or five of us dodging about the field, with the wild cow wheeling and darting in hot pursuit. Shouting and waving her arms she climbed over the gate and ran towards us intending, no doubt, to give us the sharp end of her tongue. For some reason, known only to herself, the wild cow, catching sight of Mrs Andy heading in her direction, did a spectacular U-turn and charged with alarming ferocity in the direction of her irate owner. At first Mrs Andy seemed unaware that she was the target and the pair continued towards each other on a collision course. Mrs Andy's scream when she realised what was actually happening and that she was now the prey brought a cheer from us all, now that the pressure was off, our cries and whoops increasing in volume as she turned and sprinted for the gate, arms jerking and pumping like those of an Olympic runner. There was a flash of stocking-clad legs, the sight of an enormous pair of red flannel drawers, as she almost somersaulted over the gate; and the wild cow was skidding to an abrupt halt as if suddenly aware of the enormity of the grave mistake she had just made.

As the cow ambled off Mrs Andy shouted in our direction. It was too far away for us to hear everything she said although 'young devils' and 'cheeky monkeys' and 'teacher' were sufficient to give us the general tenor of her parting statement. She arrived at school a couple of hours later. Miss Milne, summoned from the classroom by her sister, went into the cloakroom to confer with her. The door was slightly ajar so it was possible to see the two figures standing in front of the stove. Mrs Andy appeared to be doing a great deal of gesticulating and on one occasion she smacked her palms together with a resounding crack. At this Miss Milne nodded her head. When she returned, and the creaking and rattling of Mrs Andy's bicycle on the path beneath the windows had faded, she was grim-faced. It was obvious that her 'Lochgelly' was about to be summoned to her aid. Within minutes she had all the culprits standing in front of her desk. We were each given two extremely hard cracks with the strap and berated for being cheeky to Mrs Andy and for frightening her cow. If we ever did such a thing again and she got to hear about it, she said, there would be more strapping, much more, and the threat of further consequences of an unspecified nature.

Of course we did do it again, after a suitable time had elapsed, but Miss Milne obviously never got to hear about it. She never mentioned the subject again and that evening when I went, as usual, to Glebe Farm to collect the milk, heart beating somewhat wildly at the thought of confronting Mrs Andy, all she said was,

'I expect your hands will be sore tonight.'

I nodded and there was a twinkle of amusement in her tired, old eyes. But when she had filled the milk pails and I was ready for off she handed me a huge slice of bread spread thickly with fresh butter and blackcurrant jam.

'There now,' she said, 'eat that on the way home. It'll help to keep you out of mischief – for a wee while, at least.'

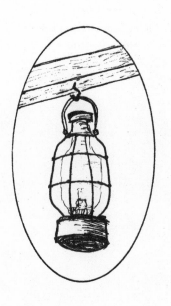

11

In 1951 electricity came to all parts of the district, the tall poles striding across fields, through clearings cut in the plantations and forests, sprouting in the back gardens of cottages, looming stark and forbidding against the limitless moorland sky. Cables were slung across deep gorges in the river and at one place where the water charged angrily along the bed of a massive ravine the work involved in slinging the stout cables from one bank to the other took the best part of a week to achieve after a series of mishaps.

Before electricity was installed in virtually every house on the estate (a few remote moorland cottages were not included) only those who lived immediately adjacent to the main road were able to use it, together with the Big House and the cottages clustered around it. In all the other houses, including mine, lighting was by paraffin lamps; softly glowing Aladdins with tall, elegantly curved chimneys or Tilleys with glowing mantles that hissed and spluttered when the pressure fell and the light began to fade. Vigorous pumping was then necessary to put fresh life into the ailing lamp and for a time banish the deepening shadows in various corners of the room. Moving around the house required the carrying of a lamp and for this purpose an Aladdin stood on the kitchen table, ready-lit with the flame turned low.

For outdoor use, visits to the woodshed, locking up the hens for the night, attending to a bitch giving birth to puppies, milking the goats, a hurricane lamp, the glass around the wick protected by a stout wire cage, was carried aloft by means of a strong handle. Even on the wildest winter's night when gales, knife-sharp from the North Sea, raged among the trees and flattened clothing to the shape of one's body, the flame in the sturdy hurricane lamp never varied. Even if upset and rolled over time and again by the force of the wind, the hurricane lamps invariably stayed alight. They were to be found in use on every farm, hanging on a nail above the stalls as the cows were being milked or, almost always in the coldest, darkest hours of the night, calves were born. At the hall a cupboard in one of the cloakrooms was set aside for storing the hurricane lamps used by those who had come on foot to attend a dance or some other function. As a result of this abundance of lamps every house, cottage and farmhouse had its own individual smell of paraffin; a friendly, welcoming smell mingling with the aroma of woodsmoke, the tobacco from a smouldering pipe, the sweet scent of furniture polish; a smell that was an everyday part of life, passing unnoticed and rarely, if ever, commented upon.

In its wake the electricity brought a new fashion in radio sets. Until then, most houses possessed a large, cumbersome radio – always referred to as 'the wireless' – heavy with knobs on its fretwork front, the dial glowing with a faint green or orange light when switched on. This was a constant source of wonderment to me, due to the plethora of exciting names – Hilversum, Lyons, Rome, Moscow, Luxembourg, Nice, Brussels, among them. Idle moments were transformed into voyages of discovery and delight as the control knob was turned and the marker-band jerked unsteadily along the dial to produce an intriguing babble of foreign voices, wisps of classical music and shreds of dance band music, most tinged with an eerie underlay of static which hissed and squeaked, popped and crackled as if relayed to one's ears from some distant planet.

Power came from one, sometimes two, accumulators brimful with acid, standing on a tray in a compartment alongside the set.

These accumulators, or 'wet' batteries as they were referred to by most people, required to be recharged at periodic intervals. This was done in Forres at the premises of a cycle repair shop, the accumulators duly labelled with their owner's name and address being transported to and from the town in a special box fastened alongside the engine of the local bus. Should a special event be about to take place, such as a world championship boxing match (commentator, Stewart Macpherson with inter-round summaries by W. Barrington Dalby), great was the rush to ensure that the accumulators were fully charged and ready for action.

I was fortunate. We had two radio sets. One was the usual accumulator model, but the other, the envy of some of my schoolfriends, was a Pye portable with a huge flat 'dry' battery the size of a small box to give it power. This meant I could take the set with me when I wanted privacy in which to listen to Aunty Kathleen's *Children's Hour* from Glasgow or Uncle Mac from London bringing me the latest instalment of an Angus MacVicar serial like *The Black Wherry* or *The Crocodile Men* with, among other riches, *Toytown* and *Ballet Shoes* and the methodical investigations of Norman and Henry Bones. Or, late in the evening, in the darkness of my bedroom, with the wind moaning and sending the rambler rose against the wall to scratch at the window while I huddled beneath the blankets cowering in terror, there came the voice of Valentine Dyall oozing sinister menace as he related the latest happenings to befall *The Man in Black*.

At first it was a strange novelty being able to move easily around the house after dark, especially during the long winter nights. Switching lights on and off became a game, running up and down the stairs with Chuffy barking at my heels, a new and enjoyable form of play previously denied us both because of the necessity to carry an Aladdin lamp or a candle in one hand. I was constantly being scolded for leaving lights burning unnecessarily and warned about the perils of wasting this positive benefit that had transformed all our lives.

Not everyone in the community saw electricity as either a blessing or a benefit, however, especially some of the elderly and penny-pinching farmers. The idea of having instant light available in byre and barn, tractor shed, stable and hen house, as well as in the farmhouse itself, horrified some to the point of obsession. There was one who admitted to having nightmares just thinking about the arrival of quarterly bills; and another, a tenant farmer, where the cost of installing the wiring and fittings had been borne by the estate, issued strict instructions to his wife, family and workers that it was not to be used under any circumstances. They had managed well enough without it in the past, he maintained, as had his father and grandfather before him. Paraffin lamps and candles had served them all well and he saw no reason to go lining the pockets of faceless individuals in a far-off town for the use of a new-fangled commodity over which he had no direct control.

For several years until he died his wife and two daughters and the two hired hands continued to do their early morning and evening chores with Aladdin, candle and hurricane lamp, while the old farmer developed a passionate hatred of the Electricity Board, cursing them long and loudly for sending him bills for the quarterly standing charge. His behaviour was a persistent source of embarrassment to his wife as the rest of the neighbourhood laughed at his antics and called him a gormless old fool. As if to spite him, as he lay in his coffin in the sitting-room and relatives and neighbours arrived to pay their last respects, his widow ceremoniously switched on all the lights in the house and surrounding farm buildings. A blaze of light from every window went stabbing into the dark February night. At once the farm became a welcoming oasis twinkling like a beacon against the sombre blackness of the surrounding moor.

'Old George would have a fit if he could see all that light,' said one man trudging down the track with some friends towards the illuminated farmhouse.

'Oh aye,' said another, pointing to the stars in the frosty sky. 'I expect he's up there now ranting and raving, busy counting the cost of his own wake.'

In the same winter that the electricity arrived was one of the worst gales that anyone had ever experienced. It started on the last day of January as a low, whispering wind with just enough strength to lift granules of snow from the surface of frozen fields and send them whirling through the air in search of fresh resting places. Until then there had been the usual amount of snow; insufficient to cause alarm, merely general inconvenience. Throughout the winter months snow always came and went with monotonous regularity. At least it never quite disappeared at any time between November and the end of March. For most of this period the night temperatures remained below freezing point so, in places, against dry-stone walls, under hedges, on the banks of the roads and in the corners of fields, the snow built up in layers to provide a permanent covering.

At first, on this particular January day there was little sign of any danger; few hints that anything out of the ordinary lay in store for us. But towards dusk snow began to fall, the first for several days, and the wind strengthened. By darkness a dense blizzard had brought visibility to almost nil, the snowflakes, plump and soft and wet, being blown madly across the face of the land to pile into drifts against any and every obstruction. At the back door of the house the snow was deep enough to reach my ankles. By mid-evening and time for bed it had reached the top of my wellington boots and little Chuffy, lured away from her fireside sleeping place by hints of a game, vanished in a flurry of snow when tricked into charging outside whenever the door was opened. By now the wind was making a peculiar noise among the tops of the surrounding trees; a low, angry, sighing sound, mingled uneasily with the noise of creaking branches and straining limbs.

In bed, in the darkness, the noise of the gale was even more sinister. Doors rattled as draughts ran riot in passages and stairway. The sprawling rose next to my window was in a frenzy against the panes, demonic fingers scratching and scrabbling incessantly across the glass. By midnight the sound of the wind was an all-pervading howl. Even inside the house I could hear the savage force of the gale among the trees, a relentless rumbling, ebbing and swelling, growling, then roaring; and when I got out of bed to press my nose against the window there was nothing but swirling snow to be seen and away, high above, a glimpse of a pale, almost shamefaced moon revealed for an instant among the flying banks of cloud.

In the morning when I awoke the blizzard had stopped, but the gale was as ferocious as ever. When I came into the kitchen for breakfast my father, who had been up and about for some time, was telling my mother about the number of trees uprooted and thrown to the ground overnight. The drive was blocked on both sides of the house and a small wooden hen house with about two dozen birds inside had been torn from its foundations and blown away, to be smashed against a pine tree in the middle of a neighbouring field. Several hens had been killed, while others had been frozen to death in the deep snow. The fittest had managed to make their way back to the shelter of the outbuildings and were, at present, huddled together in a tumbledown shed used for storing firewood.

'No school for you today, my lad,' said my father. 'It's too dangerous in this gale.'

I made no protest. The news on the radio was of disasters at sea, of ships foundering in gigantic waves or being swept headlong on to rocks, of mountain villages isolated by deep snow drifts, of the lives of towns and cities disrupted by snow, falling trees and flying masonry. Somehow the news from the outside world, and my father's words concerning what was happening in our remote corner of it, made me feel truly a part of a national emergency. I would make the most of it; enjoy the excitement while it lasted. My mother spooned more porridge (which I loathed) into my bowl as, she stressed, an added precaution against the intense cold. I heaped sugar (which I loved) on top of it and supped half-heartedly, managing to cheer myself a little with thoughts of a day of freedom away from the classroom.

At first I was told to stay indoors, but there were paths to be cut through the snow. The spaniels were barking, registering their disapproval at having to wait to be fed; the two nanny goats were bleating inside their shed; from the main hen house (still in one piece) there were squawks of discontent and occasional bursts of demented crowing from an imprisoned cockerel. I was allowed out to help my father and shortly afterwards my mother left her cooking and washing, cleaning and dusting, donned boots and an old army greatcoat and joined us shovelling snow into the teeth of the gale.

My efforts were rewarded. Eventually, I was given permission to go exploring with the proviso that I was not to go too far away from the vicinity of the house and to stay in the fields out of reach of any falling trees. This was hopeless. After a short time spent floundering around in the drifts of snow wreathing one field bordering the drive I grew tired and bored. I could see the trees at the edge of the wood bending and swaying and hear the roaring rush of the gale passing through them. I longed to be in there, too, somewhere in the heart of all the noise and vivid sensation.

I climbed over the fence and ran for the cover of the wood. Among the trees the force of the wind was less severe at ground level, but above my head amid the threatening canopy provided by the branches of oak and beech, pine and spruce, it was as if an express train was rushing past at breakneck speed. There were sounds of groaning and moaning, wailing and shrieking, sighing and whispering, caused by the constant movement of the trees lashing each other. Flurries of snow, whipped up by the wind, spun off the field and sped past to plaster themselves like icing sugar against the tree trunks. The wood was full of hollows, with thickets of rhododendron. I ran from tree to tree until I found a suitable clump. Burrowing my way beneath the drooping branches I crouched on the dry, bare floor of the wood; and waited.

What I was waiting for was neither obvious nor apparent at the time. All I knew was that if you waited, hidden and silent, in a wood for long enough you were bound to see things; and that things did happen. Woodland birds and other creatures, who may have been alarmed by your initial presence among them, usually forgot all about you in a remarkably short time. And that was when your patience and perseverance were invariably rewarded. That morning, hidden by the encircling rhododendron through which I peered with inquisitive eyes, my head filled with the anger of the wind, my patient vigilance was rewarded.

Two roe deer, a buck and a doe, came into view, nervous and silent, threading their way between the trees in hesitant bursts of movement. The constant noise and force of the wind was clearly alarming them, affecting their keen sense of hearing and even more sensitive sense of smell. They slowed and came towards the bush where I crouched hardly daring to draw breath. Only a few feet away and almost level with my eyes both animals halted, sniffing the air, their flanks rippling with nervous energy each time a new and sudden noise, the breaking of a branch, the creaking of a tree, alarmed them.

The buck's head went back to scratch at his shoulders with the points of his stubby antlers. I had a close view of his creamy-white throat stretched tight, then the doe came closer and nuzzled his neck. While doing this she grunted softly and the buck, forgetting his scratching, lowered his head to press his snout against her side. He then pawed the ground several times and performed an intricate dance, like the steps of a jig, before arching his head once again. But this time it was not to scratch. A gruff and extremely loud bark, sharper and more ominous than that of a dog, was followed by several more in rapid succession; and each time they were repeated they sounded more sinister. I had often heard deer barking, at a distance, in the woods around my home. On a dark, winter's night it could be a frightening and eerie experience; but at close range, despite my being able to see the animal, it was a sound that made me tremble. This bout of barking seemed to galvanise the doe into movement. Imitating her mate's pawing of the earth, she hopped and jumped around him, kicking her hind legs in the air, twitching her rump every so often, looking behind her as if to assess the buck's reaction to this display.

In a single movement the buck bounded forward and jumped on her back, gripping her sides with his powerful front legs. Both animals started to grunt and sway gently from side to side, moving forwards a little, backwards now and then. I had seen dogs mating, the bulls on various farms mounting their harem of cows, rams in a frenzy tupping the eager ewes, a stallion grappling with a mare in what seemed to be a violent display of ill temper; but such was the privileged feeling I had to be witness to the coupling of two of the shyest and most secretive creatures of the woods, that I felt like a furtive intruder.

It may have taken two minutes; it may have been five, or even ten. I lost all sense of time as I watched. But in that space of time I was unaware of the roaring of the wind and of the sounds of destruction it left in its wake. There, in the middle of the storm I was locked in an intimate, private world and never before had I been able to remain so quiet or so still although every minute I seemed to want to cough, or sneeze, or simply stretch my aching limbs. When it was over the two deer simply vanished from view in the space of several seconds. I watched their white tails bobbing as they trotted side by side towards the edge of the field, then turn to climb uphill to where a densely packed plantation of young conifers would provide them with shelter away from the gale and the snow.

As I stood up there was a shriek as a fierce, sustained gust of wind tore a shallow-rooted pine from the ground and sent it toppling into the branches of its neighbours. This set off a chain reaction among the trees closest to the field. Within seconds others were falling, smashing and tearing through surrounding foliage, bringing weaker trees tumbling with them, thumping and shattering on the frozen ground in a cacophony of splintering and snapping, earth and stones and the snaking tendrils of twisted roots exposed to view.

I scrambled from my hiding place and fled from the wood as the trees continued to fall. Within seconds I was pulling myself over the fence, gashing a hand on the barbed wire, then floundering in the snow-covered field. Behind me the terrible sound of destruction went on, with the shrieking and howling of the wind now like some long, sustained cry of pain. Some distance out in the field I stopped to look back. The gale had sliced a vast semicircular swathe from the wood, sending dozens of trees tumbling inwards like a fallen deck of cards. As I watched some more trees were bowled over and the gap increased, the wind probing and burrowing far into the heart of the wood. Clouds of snow were whipped from the surface of the field and sent flying among the debris of the fallen trees. Frozen granules spattered my face, stinging my cheeks. I turned and raced for home. Fresh snow was starting to fall, the huge, wet flakes tossing and turning in the wind. At the back door of the house my mother was brushing them away with the resigned air of someone trying to halt the relentless progress of an incoming tide.

'Your father says we're in for a fresh storm,' she said.

'I don't doubt it,' I replied, looking upward with the practised air of someone who could read the behaviour of the weather from the changing mood of the sky. Instead, all I got was a shower of slippery, extremely cold snowflakes on my upturned face. By mid-afternoon it was snowing steadily, the gale was worse than ever and even I, always in search of a fresh adventure, had no wish to leave the warmth of the fireside for the Arctic conditions outside. Sometime during the evening the gale died down to a blustering breeze, but the snow came spinning earthwards without a break. Throughout the night it went on falling, only stopping a short while before dawn. When I pulled open the door to go outside there was a huge drift against it, running the full length of the wall as high as the window ledges. An acute and eerie silence permeated the atmosphere. No bird sang; no cockerel crowed haughtily from the shelter of the outbuildings. Far away on a distant farm a dog barked monotonously, the sound echoing across the fields and the valley, drifting into oblivion on the moor. To me, apart from my breathing, it was the only living sound I could hear upon the face of an exhausted and ravaged land.

There was to be no school for the rest of that week. Every driveway on the estate was either blocked by drifts of snow or by fallen trees. All the surrounding roads leading to farms or on to the moors were impassable. The main road was also closed for a couple of days, then reduced to a fraction of its normal width as it ran between high walls of snow thrown up by the massive ploughs forcing their way through. Only the trains on their long climb across the moorland gave any real indication that indeed there was another world beyond our own sealed and white-coated landscape with its perpetual chilling frost and sinister wind, soughing gently through the torn and mutilated woods.

It was several days before the postman was able to call again, his little red van slithering and sliding on chain-wrapped wheels from one isolated house to the next. Farmers spent exhausting days and night digging out sheep from drifts of snow in the fields close to the farm buildings where the animals had been brought from the uplands at the onset of winter. Pheasants and pigeons flocked into gardens and raided the cabbages and kale; and foxes were seen in broad daylight close to houses and in farmyards running free with squawking hens clutched firmly in their jaws. Many of the pools on the river were frozen over and snow lay thickly on top of the ice. Here and there the gurgling of water betrayed the presence of the torrent beneath the ice and the tracks of otters and the occasional bones of a fish were reminders of the struggle for survival amid the white, hostile world in which, for a time, we were all imprisoned.

For three days the magical electricity was no more, the result of cables having been brought down by falling trees and branches. Candles and paraffin lamps were removed from cupboards and sheds and pressed into use once again. Even those foolhardy enough to have disposed of their lamps still had a supply of candles to hand. What had once been an accepted everyday task, filling the lamps, trimming the wicks, fitting new mantles, was now a great deal of fuss and bother, according to my mother. Hardly an hour went past without her testing a switch in order to check if the power had been restored.

When, once again, I made my way to school I walked across fields that resembled the frozen wastes of the Arctic. We huddled around the huge cast-iron stove in the cloakroom comparing stories of how deep the snow was around our respective houses and embellishing stories of our experiences – and those of our parents – during the worst excesses of the storm. Miss Milne warmed us all with mugs of steaming cocoa and later, in a semicircle around the piano, we sang hymns and she offered a prayer of thanks for our survival amid the rigours of gale and frost and blinding snow.

The snow and the ice were to remain for many weeks, frozen

solid by the low temperature and the ceaseless attention of the raw north wind. When, eventually, in April the frost lifted and the thaw arrived it started to rain. The rain went on falling for ninety-six hours without a break, a torrential downpour of the kind probably experienced by Noah when he made haste in building his Ark. The snow melted rapidly on the hills and on the moors; the level of the water in the river rose at an alarming speed. Within twenty-four hours we were experiencing a new drama, at times more frightening and devastating than the gales and the falling snow. The river became a raging cauldron of spray and spume and brown, mud-choked water, bursting out from its normal channel in numerous places to bring floods of a kind that no-one, adult or child, had ever seen before.

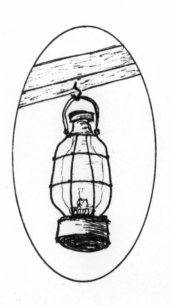

12

My father started to worry about the effect of the rain when entire trees, complete with roots and branches, began to appear in the river, hurtling downstream amid a welter of other debris in the growing torrent of water. Before long log-jams were mounting at bends in the river, causing the level to rise quickly. The water lapped the edge of the banks, then trickled over, slowly at first, gathering momentum as it surged forward in whatever direction offered the least resistance to its relentless progress.

Although our house was some distance from the river, a field and a small wood lay in between, the noise of the spate could be clearly heard, roaring and rumbling through the gorge at the foot of a tree-lined precipitous slope. I walked across the field to the top of the bank. The noise grew louder and more frightening the closer I got and when, eventually, I clung to a tree trunk and looked down at the river it was like watching and listening to the terrible anger of a giant gone totally berserk. Clouds of spray rose into the air, filtering like fine mist among the bushes and trees; and the surface of the river where once there had been a series of long, dark, placid, narrow pools, joined by rippling streams, was now a monstrous succession of foam-encrusted rapids in which not only trees but huge boulders were spinning wildly. These were smashing and tearing at the banks on either side, causing landslides of earth and rocks to plunge into the water amid explosions of mud and spray.

I watched, hypnotised, for several minutes, then fled through the teeming rain, back to the house. Once there I was scolded by my mother for getting wet, but I took little heed, my head still filled with the awesome sound of the river; and in my mind's-eye were crystal-clear images of the savagery I had witnessed. I wanted to see more. Although the raging power of the river had been frightening to see, the longer I stayed away from it the more intense became the urge which compelled me to go back. In a way I was mesmerised not only by the strength of the storm, the awful, relentless drumming of the rain on the trees and the sodden earth, but by the violence it had unleashed in the river, the results of which were clearly audible like the sustained cacophony produced by a massive thunderstorm. It might have been frightening, but it was a fear tinged with the spice of excitement. Once the urge to go back to the river was firmly implanted within me I grew more restless watching the rain streaming down the windows and hearing the constant, distant roar. Nothing could have stopped me once my mind was made up.

My mother tried.

'You must be daft,' she said as I donned an old oilskin jacket belonging to my father, so large that it served me as a full-length coat, and pulled on my wellington boots. 'You'll just get soaked to the skin and catch pneumonia,' she added, at the same time jamming her own sou'wester hat on my head and tying it firmly beneath my chin.

'No I won't,' I protested. But she was right. I did.

Not just ordinary pneumonia, which would have been bad enough, but double pneumonia, thus sentencing me to week after week and month upon month of abject misery enduring a creeping illness where each day brought fresh fevers, worse than before, and increasing weakness. I was sentenced to lie, choking and coughing, my chest clamped in a vice-like grip, for some time growing weaker by the hour, so that my only memories became hazy visions of worried faces staring down at me, the hands of my mother wiping the sweat from my burning face and chest and the fingers of the doctor checking the beat of my pulse. Even when the persistent fevers had subsided the deadly symptoms of the pneumonia held me captive in bed; and I lived on a diet of goat's milk, cod-liver oil and eggs in an effort to gain sufficient strength to overcome the debilitating effect of the illness still lingering on in the depths of my chest.

I became a prisoner in my bedroom, for a long time – too long – weakened to the point that I cared very little what might happen, my waking hours enlivened by the antics of the characters in comic magazines such as *Film Fun* and *Radio Fun*, sent to me in bundles every so many weeks by a caring aunt. Otherwise, I drifted in and out of bouts of restless sleep, by day dimly aware of the sunlight and the birdsong and the sky beyond my window; and at night comforted by the glowing firelight in the grate and the dancing shadows cast by the flames across the walls and the click of my mother's knitting needles as she sat in an armchair quietly watching over me.

The months that lay ahead were to be fraught with difficulty, worry and tension for all concerned, but on that April morning as I ran through the pelting rain in the direction of the thundering river my mother's warning meant nothing to me; just one more parental stricture to be inhaled, then discarded like a puff of cigarette smoke.

In front of the Big House the river had gone mad. One hundred yards or so from the house, standing on a plateau above terraced rock gardens, the river's normal route followed through a long, gentle 'S' bend, the bank buttressed by huge rocks set in concrete at the end of a spectacular sweep of carefully tended lawn. Close to the bottom leg of the 'S' bend a large, ornamental lake had been constructed, complete with water lilies, rustic bridges and a variety of gaily plumaged ducks.

Among the reeds a pair of magnificent mute swans nested every year, driving off intruders with furious charges and angry calls, and in the clear water fat rainbow trout either lurked in the depths or sprang towards the surface when hatching flies went skittering across the ever-placid surface.

Running along a tree-lined avenue above the tennis courts at the edge of the lawn the rain slashed through the branches on to my head. The grass squelched beneath my pounding feet and in the distance I could hear the river's roar. Breaking out of the trees I now had a clear view from the terrace in front of the Big House. The lawn had vanished. So, too, had the lake. In their place was a storm-whipped sea with wave-crested water, black as peat, foaming and boiling. Coniferous trees, such as pine and spruce, with water-logged branches, were spinning wildly in the cross-currents; huge branches bobbed and dipped like a succession of wayward corks. Having torn a way through the walled bank the river was now flooding the entire frontage, the water lapping at the foot of the terraced rockery. It had also swept through the lake to return to its original course by means of the sluice from the lake. However, the former sluice, once only a yard or two wide, was now a deep gorge twenty feet across, down which trees were rushing and boulders were rolling, sometimes being tossed into the air as if they were golf balls. The sight was so shocking and so amazing, the noise so powerful, that all I could do was stand and gape, oblivious of the rain now soaking through my coat and running down my neck inside my shirt. (Later when the rain stopped and the floodwater drained away the lawn was left pockmarked by craters and holes of varying sizes amid a carpet of silt, boulders and trunks of trees. In the holes were almost fifty salmon and scores of brown trout, most of them dead).

I ran along the path directly in front of the Big House (the laird and family were absent) towards a gate on the far side. Here, I was on the driveway again and a short distance away reached a bend in the road close to the river. At this point a rough, unmetalled road made its way across the river by way of a wooden bridge supported on four massive piles of rocks and concrete sunk deeply into the river bed. From the bridge the road, in reality no more that a pot-holed track, snaked to the right to run through several hundred yards of grassland and stunted hawthorn trees before climbing a wooded hill to reach a public road leading to the dreaded Daltullich Brae. The track was an important one; the bridge crossing saved a round trip of many miles to reach distant parts of the estate. Farmers, sometimes herding cattle, forestry workers, shepherds with flocks of sheep, my father and many others, used it. The journey to my grandparents' house was more than halved by taking the route across the bridge.

But when I ran down the short incline and on to the wooden superstructure it was perfectly clear, even to me, that soon it would be no more; very soon, I thought, as I heard the timbers creaking and groaning and felt the pulsations under my feet as thousands of tons of rushing water crashed against the piles. The bridge stood about thirty feet above the river which normally flowed swiftly, but placidly, beneath it. Now there was a log-jam of trees swaying and heaving against it where their branches and trunks had become wedged in its two neat arches. And the water now lapped within inches of the roadway, in occasional spasms flowing directly on to it. To look upstream from the middle of the bridge was an awesome and frightening sight. A solid wall of seething, roaring water rushed headlong towards me, bringing with it more debris; the bodies of sheep, twisting and turning, planks of wood, rose bushes, swathes of herbaceous plants, more trees, complete with branches and roots; and finally, minutes before the final collapse, an entire hen house with several sodden birds clinging like shipwrecked survivors to its battered roof. As yet more debris became trapped, spray rose into the air in a great cloud of fine mist and there were ominous rumbling noises from far below, directly beneath me. I felt the entire bridge ripple and twist and saw a huge chunk of masonry from one of the piles fall into the foaming water. I raced for the safety of the bank.

I stood sheltering from the rain beneath the branches of an enormous beech tree and watched part of the floor of the bridge lifted clear of the piles. It moved up and down several times, shuddering and shaking, heaving and straining; and each time it thudded back into place long cracks appeared in the roadway adjoining it. It was at this point that I heard the sound of a car engine on the far bank. Moments later I saw my father's old Ford shooting brake, which he now used for estate work instead of a bicycle, come creeping along the track and turn the corner to approach the bridge. I stepped out from against the trunk of the beech and waved. But my father didn't see me. He was too busy concentrating and deciding whether to take the risk of crossing. I could see Bess, one of his spaniels, perched in her usual place on the front seat.

I heard the engine revving and at once the Ford shot forward and on to the planks of the bridge. What happened after that took place so quickly that almost in the space of time it took to blink an eyelid, the bridge vanished. But one image, as if a camera shutter had frozen, was imprinted on my brain; the sight of the battered Ford, with my father and his dog inside, clinging to the short hill a few yards away from where I stood while behind there was first an explosion of water, trees and the entire framework of the bridge rising into the air, then a yawning divide between the banks, with the river roaring on unimpeded. The hen house went past like a ship in full sail. A solitary hen remained on top, wings drooping, drenched by the rain and the floodwater, head lolling in the final stages of abject terror.

The shooting brake went jerking past me and on to the level driveway. My father got out. So, too, did Bess. They were both drenched. He looked back to the spot where the bridge had once stood.

'My God,' he said. 'That was a close thing.'

Then he motioned me to get into the Ford. I shared the front seat with Bess. I put my arms around her neck. A rich, heavy smell of earth and wet leaves rose from her warm, damp body. She turned her head towards me and pressed her muzzle against my cheek. I was surprised to find I was shaking. Throughout the journey home my father said not another word. Once indoors he poured himself a whisky, then another, while my mother admonished me severely for allowing myself to be soaked to the skin.

My father drank a third glass of whisky and while I was upstairs changing into dry clothes I heard his voice starting to tell of what had almost happened to him. When I got back to the kitchen he was laughing about his adventure, although judging by the expression on my mother's face she considered the episode to be far from funny. Plates were being placed on the table and when the lid of a pot on the stove was lifted a tantalising aroma of beef and onions and carrots made me suddenly feel happy again; and hungry.

'Now,' she said, ladling a huge pile of stew on to my plate, 'eat that or you catch your death of cold.'

But, as I've ready indicated, I nearly did. A week or so later I was in bed with the first symptoms of pneumonia starting to show themselves. The sun was shining weakly from a watery sky overburdened by bank upon bank of ominous clouds. The floodwater started to subside and the river returned to its normal level; and, where appropriate, to its former course. But the estate was devastated; hundreds of acres of fallen trees, driveways closed, farm tracks washed away, fields damaged, fences wrecked, livestock killed or seriously injured. It was to take months, if not several years, to fully repair the damage. In some places it was never put right. And for the rest of my childhood there were areas of fallen trees and parts of the river banks as constant reminders of the worst storm ever since 1855.

But the most permanent reminder of all was that image in my head of the bridge exploding in a cascade of water and timber behind the little Ford shooting brake just as it reached the bank. And of my father's face, grey behind the rain-washed windscreen; and of his knuckles, white and straining, as with both hands he gripped the steering wheel and drove himself and old Bess to safety.

13

My favourite part of the entire estate was the moorland. Amid the empty acres where the distant horizon merged with the encircling sky, there was stillness; and peace; and a great sense of boundless freedom.

Other areas were, perhaps, more beautiful in that they had been planned; forests of oak and beech, larch and pine; well-maintained driveways running through woods and alongside fields with grazing cattle or growing oats and barley, potatoes and turnips; the formal gardens with their high stone walls against which flourished plums and pears, damsons and apples and, in the sunniest spots, fat, ripe peaches with a taste so magnificent it was well worth taking the risk of incurring the head gardener's wrath in order to raid and plunder, then gorge oneself full. There were also massive greenhouses, faintly sinister with their aura of sticky humidity and moist, rich compost in which lurked geraniums wafting a sickly scent, cloying like incense, amid drooping ferns and row upon row of potted chrysanthemums. Massive vines with both black and green grapes writhed across a part where the connecting door was always padlocked when the bunches hung in heavy clusters and the final stages of ripening began; and tomatoes, countless dozens of plants, both red and yellow, on which the fruit was so abundant the trusses were supported by strands of thick wire.

Behind one corner of the walled gardens was a wooded hill, about 200 feet high; and on its summit the crumbling remains of a thirteenth-century castle. As it was surrounded by what had been a natural moat, now a deep gorge overgrown with oak and hazel, larch and birch, the feeling of isolation gained by climbing to the top was both overpowering and rich in dramatic possibilities. There was still sufficient of the castle remaining to make it an exciting and unusual place to explore; parts of walls with arrow-slit windows, a couple of arches, a fragment of winding staircase which ended abruptly in front of a large window high on the tallest remaining wall, to give a clear view of the river and the wooded hills beyond.

More exciting than anything else, however, was the underground chamber with one narrow window cut into the rock through which, by craning your neck, it was possible to see straight down the steep bank and into the bed of the gorge. Leading off from this chamber was a passage which wound its way down through dank, sour-smelling earth in a series of tight spirals of alarming tenuity due to the rapid rate of descent. This tunnel was reputed to sink beneath the bed of the moat before running for a further half-mile to emerge in a cave some way up the face of a ravine in the middle of what was now a pine forest.

I lost count of the number of times I went down the passage, heart thumping, slipping on the beaten-earth floor, stumbling over fallen rocks, stubbing my toes on partly buried steps which had been sunk in the more difficult sections; trying, always trying, to follow the subterranean route to wherever it might lead me. Water constantly trickled down the walls and in the light of the candle (I always kept a supply behind a loose stone in the chamber above my head) I was persistently challenged by slithering shadows which loomed up and lunged at me, the tendrils of long claws seeming to grasp at my body as I scurried on down like a frightened rat. Here and there on the walls were the remains of sconces which I knew from my history books had been used to hold torches of pitch. So, always, I was sure that the stories and legends surrounding the castle were indeed true; that the underground passage was a secret way in and out of the fortress on the hill. But my attempts at full exploration were constantly thwarted on the first, straight level stretch which I judged to be directly under the moat. A massive rock fall, caused by the roots of trees (which I could see) breaking through the roof, sealed off the remainder of the passage. Try as I might it was impossible for me to move any of the boulders or shift sufficient earth in order to squeeze past.

At the other end, in the cave, there was little or no fun to be gained from exploration there. It was exciting to clamber down the face of the ravine and into the cave, clinging to bushes and rocks, but once inside, having squeezed between two moss-covered boulders, there was only a short stretch of tunnel to be seen. This was at the back of a cavern festooned overhead by bats and on the floor by their evil-smelling droppings and after no more than ten or twelve feet it, too, was blocked by fallen debris. Nevertheless, I kept on visiting and exploring both places – the castle and the cave – obsessed by the idea of following the passage along its entire length; my head filled with images of men hunted and men hunting, of outlaws hiding far down in the bowels of the earth while the King's men searched the forest above and laid siege to the tiny castle perched on its mound above the river.

But when I wasn't at the castle more likely than not I would be far out on the moor, revelling in the sheer joy of being free among so much wild open space. Prior to the start of the Second World War in 1939 there had been a number of farms, their houses occupied by families of various generations from grandmother to grandson, their rough fields cultivated for potatoes and turnips, sometimes even a smattering of oats. Sheep grazed whatever pasture there was to graze and found additional sustenance in grassy pockets among the heather. Now, most of these houses were empty, some in ruins, almost totally derelict, the rafters bare after the removal of the roofing slates, the exposed timbers gleaming white like the bones of some stranded fish, now decayed. Beneath the foundations of one such raddled farmhouse foxes had made a den and cubs played among the tangled fruit bushes of the overgrown garden or sunned themselves in the old sheep pens where the grass was a ripe, dark green and two feet high.

The few moorland farms still in general use were those on the fringe of the moor where the pasture was rich enough to support herds of beef and milk cattle and the loam was of a quality that would produce crops of oats and barley with a yield only marginally less than that achieved on the lowland farms. There was, however, one farm, in reality only a croft, which was still inhabited and this was spectacularly isolated from its neighbours and the rest of the estate. Old Mrs MacDonald lived there, tenant of the place after the death of her husband who had combined working the land with a job as a permanent way labourer on the nearby railway line. When her grandson Donald left home to seek a job she was left alone, four miles from the nearest house; alone at the end of a rough and ready track which forded one river and one small burn and crossed the railway line before winding a weary path through the heather to arrive at her cottage nestling in a hollow between two small hills. She was alone, but always appeared perfectly content as she found jobs to do among her goats, hens and various hives of bees.

I loved the spot where she lived. There was a quality of peace and tranquillity about both house and surroundings that conveyed itself powerfully and convincingly even to the barely formed inner soul of a twelve-year-old. She had a black and white collie, a typical sheepdog, called Jess and I marvelled at the capacity of this dog to understand all that was required of her. When Mrs MacDonald wanted fresh meat from the butcher she gave a letter to the postman who cycled up and down the rough track to her home. It was an arduous job for him, especially in the winter months, but his visits to the house were well rewarded in the shape of bowls of hot soup, plates of stew and cups of tea. He, in turn, sent it on to a relative of hers in Grantown-on-Spey. She went to the butcher and gave the list of requirements to him; and when the order was ready collected the parcel neatly wrapped with brown paper and string. She then handed it in to the railway station in the town where, of course, Mrs MacDonald's husband had been well known during his years of service looking after the track. At this stage the parcel was given to the guard on a suitable train who informed the engine driver and fireman that there was a parcel to deliver to Mrs MacDonald. The meat was now ready to embark on a fourteen-mile journey to her home.

When the train emerged from a deep cutting about half a mile away from her house the engine driver sounded his whistle, a mutually prearranged signal. It was now time for Jess to swing into action. Without the need of any command from Mrs MacDonald the collie would race across the small fields with their rushes and rough grass, swim across the burn, pick her way through a patch of marshland, where in spring gulls and plovers nested and reared their young, bounding helter-skelter, tongue lolling and breathless, to be at the boundary fence alongside the track almost as the train came level and went past. Curious passengers looked up from their books, newspapers or knitting or came awake as they felt the brakes applied and the train, previously running fast on the downhill gradient, jerked a little, couplings clanking, and slowed to almost a walking pace. Those lucky enough to see the reason for the change in speed were treated to the sight of a small brown parcel spinning through the air over the fence to land in the heather, usually directly in front of Jess's nose. At once she would pick it up by a loop in the string and bound away homewards; and in the far distance, somewhere near the door of the small, squat house with its smoking chimney, no matter the weather, a diminutive figure would be waving a handkerchief as the whistle of the engine sounded a couple of blasts and the train picked up speed and disappeared from view as if nothing untoward had happened.

Over the years Jess made similar journeys on hundreds of occasions carrying, in addition to meat, bottles of brandy, cough mixture and pills from the chemist, newspapers and magazines, balls of knitting wool and, from time to time, fresh fruit such as oranges and bananas, each parcel done up in the traditional way with its loop of string so that the faithful dog could carry it between her teeth. Only once did an accident occur. A bottle of brandy, a favourite remedy, required to aid Mrs MacDonald's recovery from a bout of 'flu, struck a stone when flung from the train and shattered. When Jess arrived back at the cottage the paper was sodden and reeking of alcohol. The collie's lips were wrinkled, twisted back, her nostrils twitching, as she gripped the string attached to the bundle of paper and broken glass. Normally she waited patiently until a parcel was taken from her. This time she dropped the remnants at Mrs MacDonald's feet and raced off.

'Oh, Jess,' she said, 'now I know you've got no taste for drink.'

Inside Mrs MacDonald's small house, with its thick, stone walls and tiny windows, the atmosphere was as friendly and welcoming as she was herself. Most of the fuel in the permanently burning fire was peat, cut into slabs from an area near the house, and pieces of branches dragged from the remains of a wood on the side of one of the hills. The trees had been felled during the Second World War, but only the best timber was extracted leaving for years to come a rich supply of firewood to warm Mrs MacDonald and Jess. When it came to peat cutting, the best time being June or early July when, hopefully, the slabs would dry quickly in the hot sun, Mrs MacDonald was perfectly capable of doing the job herself. But my father and some of the other workers on the estate usually did most of it for her when they were on the moor cutting their own supply for the winter months. It was a small token of his thanks for the hot tea and even hotter soup from a huge pot, kept simmering on her shining, black-leaded range, which she gave to him on freezing winter days when for one reason or another he found himself up on the moor.

Every time my father went to the area of moorland surrounding her home he called at the shop where Mattie would have a grocery order ready, the list having been brought to her earlier in the week by the postman who, in turn, sent word to my father that Mrs MacDonald was in need of fresh supplies. In this way, tea, sugar, biscuits, candles and paraffin (among many other items) all found their way to her house. Now and then she would leave her home and set off down the track, crossing the railway line and wading the fords, pushing an ancient bicycle with a wicker basket on the handlebars and two pannier bags on either side of the rear wheel. In this fashion when the mood took her and the weather was good she would ferry her own groceries home. But she never rode the bicycle. Even on the main roads she pushed it, a black hat with a splendid feather on its crown on her head, a black coat wrapped around her slight, frail body, even in summer, and what can best be described as huge, sensible, black shoes on her feet. Although quite happy to gossip and chat with anyone she met she spent the least possible time in the shop. Business over she was off again on the return journey. By the time she was back at her house she would have walked about sixteen miles.

Mrs MacDonald loved her isolated moorland home with such a degree of strength and ferocity that to be away from it made her feel ill, she said. On one occasion she had to go to hospital in Inverness for an operation. It was the first time she had been away from her own house for many years. Once the surgery was completed she merely lay in bed moping and spiritless, the cause of great anxiety to my parents and others who went to visit her. After ten days or so the operation was judged a complete success, but mentally and emotionally she was only a fragment of her former self. The doctors thought she would be too weak to look after herself (indeed she seemed to grow weaker each day) and because of this decided to delay her release. Fortunately, a nurse, herself from some remote croft in the Western Isles, who understood the old woman's feelings persuaded them to let her go home despite her frailty. When she was given the news it was the first time a smile had been seen on her face for over a fortnight.

A letter arrived asking my father if he would be good enough to meet her off one of the afternoon trains and take her in his shooting brake to her house. It was only four days since he had last seen her sitting up in her hospital bed. Afterwards, on the way home, there had been gloomy talk of the poor state she had been in.

When we stood on the station platform as the train steamed in, hissing and clanking, her wrinkled face was already there, framed in the open window of a carriage door; sniffing the fresh air; smiling again. The transformation in her appearance and demeanour was remarkable; the smile later becoming laughter and tears when Jess was collected from the farmer who had been looking after her and the two were joyfully reunited; smiles, laughter, tears and a hug for us all, each in turn when, at last, she was back, safe at the door of her lonely home.

The crying of the curlews seemed to carry a lighter hint of melancholy that day. With the boisterous screeching of the lapwings and the poignant piping of the golden plovers the birds were as one in a chorus of welcome. And at last a lovely old woman was content and at peace once again; overjoyed to be back in a place where the birds and the roaming foxes were her daily companions and at night the moon's white light rested on her house in the hollow; the house where she'd been born and where, one day, she would be equally content to die.

14

When the elderly cook-housekeeper, the only permanent resident of the Big House for most of the year, decided to retire a succession of incumbents came and went, some filling the post for only a few months, others for one year, sometimes two. One of the most enduring was Mrs Anstruther who brought with her from some similar establishment in the wilds of the English Lake District a bad-tempered and unruly cocker spaniel and a long-legged beautiful daughter with a head of flowing hair the colour of sun-kissed straw. She was called Sarah, aged fourteen, at the time of her arrival two years older than me. From the moment of first setting eyes on her I idolised her, instantly won over by her startling good looks and soon to appreciate that she possessed a wild sense of humour, always ready for mischief and adventure.

Mother and daughter and surly dog arrived in a haze of blue exhaust smoke pouring from the rear of a tiny, highly polished, maroon-coloured Austin car. Because of their minute size such cars were lovingly described as 'baby' Austins and it was hard to see how the two occupants, plus dog and layer upon layer of luggage, could all have been fitted inside without some degree of outside help. When the doors were opened they seemed to spill forth rather than emerge. But fully aware of the incongruity of their situation they both laughed a greeting in response to my parents' welcome, while the dog sniffed at my boots, growled, and bared his teeth in my direction for the very first time.

Mrs Anstruther was a small, cheery, stout woman who, when she laughed, wobbled all over. As her sense of fun was highly developed she seemed to spend a considerable amount of time in a state of quivering motion. It made me laugh just to see her laugh. This, in turn, would make her laugh even more. All at once the staid corridors of the Big House began to echo with the sound of laughter and wherever she went around the estate she left behind her a lingering aroma of powder and scent; and the memory of that laugh which came from the depths of her ample frame and succeeded in bringing a twist to the lips of even the sourest inhabitant.

I was not long in discovering that in addition to daughter Sarah being good company, mother was a cook of great distinction. My own mother's cooking and baking was of the best. Even as a youngster I could appreciate that, although there were times when I moaned about having to eat porridge and turned up my nose at yet another bowl of vegetable-laden Scots broth, full of warmth on the coldest winter's day. But Mrs Anstruther brought a new dimension to my knowledge of cakes, puddings and other delights, previously unknown. It was not to be long before I seemed to be seeing as much of mother as I did of daughter Sarah, both being among the most pleasurable experiences I had yet encountered.

In Mrs Anstruther's capable hands gooseberries were transformed into light-as-air mouth-watering fools, raspberries became mousse, tender as silk, strawberries were topped with lashings of foaming cream fresh from the Home Farm; and a supply of rock cakes, fairy cakes, shortbread and sponges, oozing butter icing and home-made jam, flowed constantly from her oven. Whenever I went to the Big House (and my visits grew more frequent as time passed) she seemed to be in the middle of a mammoth bout of baking. Bowls and baking trays littered the enormous scrubbed table in the kitchen and even on the hottest day of summer the air surrounding the

Aga cooker shimmered and pulsated with a scorching, sweat-prickling heat.

Mrs Anstruther, wiping her florid face with flour-encrusted hands, always welcomed me with a smile. If a cake was ready it was popped directly into my mouth while a tray containing another batch was borne aloft towards the oven. I never refused one of Mrs Anstruther's offerings and the more I ate the more she seemed compelled to feed me. In a way I was almost like some nestling cuckoo always looking for more and Mrs Anstruther behaved like a surrogate parent and saw to it that my needs were met. Sarah hardly seemed to eat anything. I could never understand how she managed to keep her hands off the tantalising morsels which seemed to permanently surround her. No doubt her indifference to cakes and sponges was why she remained so slim. Wide-eyed and smiling and more often than not wearing brief, white tennis shorts, she would sit on the edge of the table dangling her fabulous legs; and the laughter of mother and daughter made the world a happier, more reassuring place.

As the laird's visits to the estate were infrequent – the longest being during the summer months and at Christmas and the New Year – this meant that Mrs Anstruther and Sarah had the rambling mansion house to themselves for much of the year; she cooking the cakes she loved (and I adored) and supervising the cleaning which was done by several wives of estate workers who came in for a few hours each day. They, too, benefited from the cakes and sponges and a morning tea break was a lavish affair much appreciated and lingered over.

When Mrs Anstruther judged I had eaten sufficient for the time being (and for each cake and portion of sponge I consumed she matched it, washing them down with great draughts of tea) I was usually despatched, with Sarah, to walk the tetchy, grumbling, growling cocker spaniel. Sarah's company I, of course, adored. The spaniel's I hated and could well have done without. Called Badger, it was the most spiteful, unruly and undisciplined dog I had ever encountered. Having grown up with spaniels, and labradors who did as they were told, walked at heel and never chased rabbits or wandering pheasants, I was horrified by Badger's behaviour. If he heard a roe deer moving away in a wood as we approached he was off, barking and yelping, ignoring all shouts to return, the sound of his pursuit of the beast marked by the hysteria of his cries, darting this way and that, then going around in circles, until he returned, breathless, but eager for more.

Both Mrs Anstruther and Sarah adored him. In their eyes he could do no wrong. They hugged and cuddled him, kissed his nose and the top of his head and crooned soft, loving words in his ears. I longed to give him a hearty kick. He never actually tried to bite me, but would rush headlong at my legs, barking all the time, and snarling, which made Sarah laugh and me swear, not always under my breath. I grew more eager to plant my boot on his curly, mud-stained backside. It became an obsession. He seemed to sense this. And when Sarah and I went out together the infuriating Badger made sure I was never given an opportunity to be alone with him. His dislike of me grew swiftly to match my loathing of him; so much so that when I visited Mrs Anstruther and Sarah in their comfortable sitting room in the Big House he remained in his basket beneath the wide bay window, snarling softly if I dared to venture too close or even looked too earnestly in his direction.

At home, from time to time, I would hear my father angrily recalling how he had seen Badger running wild in the woods near the Big House and emphasising how he would have to have words with Mrs Anstruther about her dog's behaviour. He had young pheasants to rear and protect ready for the shooting season and Badger's antics were not making life any easier for him. My mother agreed that the dog needed 'a good thrashing' to teach it how to behave and I longed for the day when my father would corner him so that the long overdue punishment might be administered. Meanwhile, he made periodic visits to the Big House to complain to Mrs Anstruther. But if the occasion on which I accompanied him was a typical example then the complaining was minimal and considerably restrained.

As cheery as ever Mrs Anstruther greeted him with a beaming smile.

'Hullo, Rod. It's the dog again. I know by the look on your face.'

'Yes,' replied my father, looking stern and forbidding. He was good at that.

'Oh dear. What are we going to do about him?' she said.

'You'll have to keep him locked up,' said my father, still wearing his grim expression.

'But I do. I do. Well, I do try,' replied the effervescent Mrs Anstruther, motioning us into the long corridor which led to her living quarters. In her sitting-room Sarah was curled up on the sofa reading a book. Badger twitched and growled in the depths of his basket.

'Sit down. Sit down,' said Mrs Anstruther. And my father sat.

'Sarah. You've upset Rod again. You must not let Badger run all over the place when you're out with him. Lead, Sarah. You must keep him on his lead.'

'Yes, Mam,' said Sarah sweetly, uncurling her long frame and stretching as she got to her feet. I could see her tummy where her blouse had pulled free from the waistband of her shorts.

'I do tell her. I do tell her,' said Mrs Anstruther to my father.

'I know you do,' he replied. His expression was now less stern and forbidding.

'It won't happen again,' said Mrs Anstruther. 'I'll make absolutely sure that Sarah puts him on a lead whenever she takes him for a walk.'

'And keeps him on the lead,' said my father.

'And keeps him on it,' said Mrs Anstruther.

I smiled. My father laughed. Badger growled deeply. Mrs Anstruther laughed. And Sarah's smile was as warm as the sun itself. Badger on a lead was a sight to behold. He went mad, bucking and straining, leaping and twisting, like a maddened pony in a Wild West rodeo. If he as much as saw a lead he disappeared into inaccessible corners or crawled beneath impenetrable bushes. But the thought was there, in Mrs Anstruther's mind; and honour was satisfied.

It was now time for Mrs Anstruther to produce a bottle of whisky and two cut-glass tumblers from her sideboard.

'You'll have a wee dram, Rod,' she said without turning her head.

'Oh aye,' he replied. 'Just a wee one.'

And promptly she filled a double measure for both of them. While Sarah and I were sent to the kitchen to get lemonade ('and don't forget to give the boy some cakes') the pair of them settled back to enjoy their whisky. And when it was time to leave Mrs Anstruther's face was a jollier hue than usual and any hint of grimness in my father's features was very much a thing of the past. There were repeated promises on Mrs Anstruther's part that Badger from now on would cause no further trouble and vague responses from my father that she wasn't to worry herself too much about it.

'Come back and see me later,' whispered Sarah in my ear. I needed no second invitation. In the kitchen between mouthfuls of lemonade and sponge, light as a feather and squelching with strawberry jam, she had kissed me on the cheek. I'd been so surprised I'd almost choked. I'd cringed with embarrassment. But Sarah had ruffled my hair and said,

'You can kiss me sometime. If you want to.'

I think I must have been gaping at her because she suddenly stood back, placed her hands on her hips and said archly,

'You do want to kiss me, don't you?'

There was nothing I wanted more. But I was too shy to say so. However, I nodded my head and this seemed to satisfy her.

'It can be a lot of fun,' she said; and there was a strange, distant expression in her lovely, green eyes. She pouted her full lips at me. 'I'd like you to kiss me.'

'What, now?' I said hoarsely. There were crumbs stuck to the roof of my mouth.

'No. Later on,' she said, skipping away across the vast room as if trying to get out of reach. She needn't have worried. I'd been given three slices of sponge. There was still one to finish. As I munched my way through it she came back and poured me some more lemonade. There was laughter from the sitting-room, my father's and Mrs Anstruther's. The faint clink of glasses. Sarah filled her own glass and stretched out on a chair. Her legs seemed to go on for ever, the shorts tight across the tops of her thighs. There were fine, golden hairs on her legs and in the space between blouse and shorts I saw more hair, just as soft and silky. Carefully and deliberately she unfastened another button and I saw her belly button, a neat indentation on the smoothness of her tummy.

Then there were voices in the corridor outside and it was time to go. But at the door I replied I'd be back in the evening and Sarah smiled and nodded and behind her mother's back blew me a kiss. Although my cheeks went red I felt an excitement of the kind I had never experienced before. But I knew what it was. I knew what had happened to me. Of course I'd been waiting for it to happen to me in the same way I knew it happened to so many other boys.

I was in love. And Sarah was in love with me.

I wasn't able to return to the Big House to see Sarah that evening. A thunderstorm, followed by several hours of heavy rain, put paid to that. Since my double pneumonia I was supposed to avoid getting wet, according to my mother. Whether it was her own ruling or the doctor's advice I never knew. But whenever it could be enforced, it was a rule to be obeyed. For some time, immediately after my recovery, at the first hint of rain my movements would be given the sort of attention a hovering kestrel usually reserves for the frenetic scurryings of a worried mouse. If I showed any inclination to go outdoors obstacles would be placed in my way (homework to do, tea almost ready, shoes to be cleaned). If I failed to take the gentle, but firm, hint my movements were then curtailed. I was confined to the house; by order. And I knew that I was beaten, once again. Like the evening following Sarah's kiss when all I could do was stay indoors, sulking a little, then sulking a lot as I stared gloomily at the falling rain.

Eventually, I quickly learned to keep an eye open for signs of a change in the weather; the formation of particular clouds, a darkening sky, a faint rumble of thunder in the distance. Although my system was far from perfect it did achieve a fair degree of accuracy so, very soon, I was able to be away from the house and well out of earshot long before any restrictions could be placed on me. In time it became too much of an effort for my busy mother to watch the weather as well as what I was up to so, after a decent interval when we both played this particular game of cat and mouse with grim determination, I was left alone and the possibility of my getting wet was never mentioned again.

During this period when I was not supposed to get wet I was swimming regularly in a pool on the moorland stretch of the river. Swimming with Sarah. No-one knew we went swimming. We just set off on our bicycles, lemonade in the saddlebags and, depending on whose day it was to be the provider, a generous quantity of either my mother's or Mrs Anstruther's cakes and sandwiches. We simply set off together as we did so often that summer (and the one that followed), two kindred spirits seeking the pleasure of each other's company, in search of what we might find or see amid the thousands of acres of moorland, forest and riverbank that was an everyday backdrop to our lives. No-one ever imagined we went swimming. How could they? Neither Sarah nor I could swim.

It was Sarah who first suggested the idea. But then, she was two years older than me. Mentally, she was on another planet, mature far in advance of her years. Even at twelve years old I could recognise signs of this maturity. And I was glad of it. When decisions had to be taken it was nice to leave them to her. She wasn't bossy. Merely firm and decisive. I was hopeless at making up my mind. When I did I was almost always wrong. Invariably, she was right. Many's the act of mischief we perpetrated together when detection was only avoided thanks to her skill in covering our tracks. She was quick to think of an answer when awkward questions fell into our laps. I was remarkably slow. But I was a willing pupil and several months in her company taught me a great deal in the art of survival. To an only child Sarah was, in many ways, the ideal elder sister with the added thrill that she loved me; loved me in the heart-pounding, stomach-turning, mouth-drying way that I experienced both in her company and away from it. I knew now, beyond a shadow of a doubt, that she loved me. It wasn't merely a much-grasped-at passing straw of fancy floating freely in the whirlpool of my daydreaming fantasies and ripe, almost limitless imaginings.

I knew because she told me so. I had heard the magical words from her very own lips. On the first day we went swimming together. And when she told me what I wanted to hear she placed a daisy chain of wild flowers, plucked from a damp, mossy grotto at the base of a waterfall, around my neck; and this time she kissed me, not on the cheek, but full square on the lips.

It was then she suggested we swim in the long, wide pool below the waterfall. We'd cycled for five or six miles to reach the spot, most of them on a bumpy, stony track threading its way in a haze of heat through boundless moorland, purple and white with the heather in flower and alive with the ceaseless calling of grouse and the soleful crying of curlew and plover. She was hot, she said. I looked hot, she said. I replied that I certainly felt hot.

'But I can't swim,' I said.

'It doesn't matter,' she replied.

I thought it mattered a great deal. I was about to say so.

'I can't swim either,' she interrupted. 'But I've always wanted to try. Haven't you?'

I'd spent twelve years beside tumbling rivers and quiet moorland lochs and never ever felt the slightest inclination to go swimming in them.

'Yes,' I said. 'Often.'

'Good,' she said. 'It wouldn't be such fun if you didn't do it too.'

'But I've nothing to wear,' I said.

She seemed to think this a crazy excuse. She laughed for some time.

'Then that makes two of us,' she said.

And with that her blouse was off and her shorts came down; her sandals were kicked to one side. I tried to look at the sky, the wind-swept trees crouching among the rocks on either bank; at my feet; anywhere but at her. There seemed to be a roaring noise in my head. My mouth had gone dry. My legs felt like rubber.

She was stark naked, tossing her long, blonde hair in the air with a playful shake of her head. I had a vague idea that girls of her age were supposed to wear brassières to contain their budding breasts. There had been one girl at school who had started to wear one before she went to the town to attend the academy. It was a topic of conversation for days for both boys and girls when she first put in an appearance with all the airs and graces of a nubile film star. But Sarah, on that day at least, had no brassière to take off. Neither was she wearing knickers. I know this really surprised me. After all I thought every girl wore those. Now and then when games became rough in the school playground I'd seen plenty glimpses of them, amid flailing arms and legs and ear-piercing screams.

'It's your turn now,' she said. 'You can't refuse. Not now. Not now that I've done it.'

One part of me wanted to refuse; another set my nerves tingling and willed me to do as she asked.

'If you love me like I love you,' she said, 'you'll do it for me.'

Even a tongue-tied, red-faced, apparently innocent twelve-year-old could not be so ungallant as to refuse such a direct, challenging request.

'I won't look while you do it,' she said. Her eyes were wide with anticipatory delight.

I stripped off my old grey shorts and slowly removed my shirt. My socks were rolled down and came off with my shoes. I hesitated momentarily when it came to my underpants. But it was too late; events had now gone too far to allow modesty to call a halt. Off they came.

I, too, was naked, just like Sarah. The sun's warmth embraced my bare body. And suddenly I didn't mind that she had broken her promise and was looking; making no pretence of peeking through outstretched fingers in front of her face, but staring boldly and frankly with the sort of smile on her face I would have followed no matter what she'd asked me to do or where she'd suggested we might go. In an instant it was all glorious, hilarious fun.

I ran towards her, laughing, and pushed her backwards into the river. Giggling and screaming she plunged out of sight beneath the water, emerging seconds later water spewing from her mouth, gasping and snorting, threshing the pool with her arms and legs. I jumped in alongside her, completely unprepared for the icy touch of the water. I, too, went under. I thought I was going to drown. Desperately, I flailed with my arms and lashed out with my legs until I broke through the surface. Then Sarah was holding on to me. We were holding on to each other. Wet bodies, slippery as eels, twisted and turned, writhed and undulated, touching and bumping with intertwined legs as we kept each other afloat; then rested, clinging to the grassy bank, each with one hand on the hard, baked earth. Our free hands encircled each other's waists, clamped firmly flesh upon flesh, with the sort of grip that says everything because in its strength is all the ferocity of the knowledge of undying love.

I forgot how cold the water was and we lingered in the pool for some time, much of it spent treading the water near the edge, enjoying the close proximity of our bodies, the smoothness of their touch, as we supported each other. Now and then we grew bolder and kicked away from the bank to bob up and down like two corks, hanging on to each other for mutual comfort and safety. I felt her small breasts rub against me so often that after a time I accepted the sight and touch of them as completely normal. And when she touched me between the legs and I felt her hand lingering there I decided instantly that I liked what was being done and made no bashful protest with lowered eyes and blushing cheeks.

On the bank we stretched out among the grass and ferns and lay, first of all on our backs and then on our stomachs, with the light of the afternoon sun dappling our bodies through the branches of the surrounding trees. I wanted to lie in the full sun to dry, but Sarah's wisdom came to the fore at once.

'Don't be daft,' she said. 'You'll get roasted. And how are you going to explain to your Mam how your bum got sunburnt?'

If she had mentioned the word 'bum' prior to our naked swim together I would have curled up with embarrassment to hear it fall from the lips of a girl. But now I just laughed and felt content. And felt more in love than ever with this blonde-haired, long-legged girl with the ability to think of things I had neither the experience nor the foresight to imagine.

We drank our lemonade, passing the bottle between us, lifting it, unwiped, to our eager lips. We ate the sandwiches and even Sarah had more than one cake. We kissed each other until my lips felt bruised; and we explored every portion of our respective bodies with inquisitive hands and probing fingers. It was a day such as I could never have imagined might happen to me. I'm sure it was the sort of day Sarah had planned. And I was glad. At the end of it we cycled home and kissed each other goodnight at a bend in the driveway before we reached my parents' house. We told each other again, for the two thousand and sixty-eighth time, that we loved each other and would never, ever, love anyone else. If we did we would surely die.

Of course, our love affair was doomed to failure right from the start. At fourteen and attending the secondary school in Forres, Sarah was of an age to attract the attentions of boys older than me and considerably more knowledgeable about love and girls and all the exciting and tantalising benefits accruing from both. At twelve years of age and still at the local primary school I was, unfortunately, still merely a youngster. Fun to be with? Yes; Sarah must have thought so. Romantic? Yes; up to a point. But my idea of romance was still confined to the amount of kissing each could manage. The logical follow-through to sex, while obviously a thought burning brightly in Sarah's mind, was something which at the time I was both unprepared mentally and unable physically to do much about. Nevertheless, throughout that first summer, during the long school holidays we repeated our nude swimming and sunbathing sessions on several occasions. Each time we both got more fun, considerably more pleasure, and with Sarah in control I'm sure I gained some experience of a kind which, at least I was certain, was still denied my fellow pupils in school.

We went on long cycle rides, played tennis on the Big House court, walked for miles together along the carefully tended paths threading their various ways through the woods and along the banks of the river. Mrs Anstruther doted on me by providing cakes in abundance and beautiful Sarah accepted my puppy-like devotion with an unrestrained display of love and eager romanticism. I longed for the day when I, too, would attend the academy. Then Sarah and I would travel to town together on the school bus. We would be able to see each other throughout the day, talk to each other at break-times (so I fondly imagined, failing to take into account that the sexes were segregated in separate playgrounds), and life would be richer and rosier than ever before.

But almost as soon as the magical day was about to dawn and I was finding it hard to contain my excitement, Sarah fell for another boy, a great, hulking lout in long trousers called George. And the betrayal was all the more savage because I found them together in the Big House kitchen and he was stuffing Mrs Anstruther's cakes into his mouth as if he had never seen food for a week, between bites and bouts of chewing praising the jolly mother for the excellence of her baking.

'This is George,' said Mrs Anstruther.

George nodded in my direction, noting my diminutive stature, the white face and narrow shoulders, the grey flannel shorts, the knee-length socks, rumpled and around my ankles. In contrast he looked the picture of good health and smartness. He smiled with the corners of his mouth. I saw it as a sneer.

'Hullo,' he said. 'Push off, kid,' is what he was thinking; what he really wanted to say.

'George cycled all the way from Forres just to see me,' said Sarah unhelpfully. Her wide eyes were shining. Raw youngster I might be, but even I could see that George was getting more than his fair share of admiring looks; and that although I was not being totally ignored I was on the way out as the prime contender for Sarah's affections. I was told by Mrs Anstruther to help myself to some cakes. But I only had one. It tasted stale. I hung about for half an hour or so, then made some feeble excuse and went home. And moped.

Sarah, however, did not drop out of my life. I was kept on as second reserve, a position I quickly grew to tolerate. After all, it was better than nothing and even George couldn't cycle the eight miles uphill all the way from Forres every Saturday or Sunday or every single day whenever the school was on holiday.

Both George and I were left high and dry at the same time. Mrs Anstruther, eager to be on the move again, found a new job in the autumn of the following year. Sarah, now even more attractive and alluring than ever, was spirited away from us, all in the space of a fortnight.

Mrs Anstruther left the estate as she had arrived: wreathed in smiles and wobbling all over with laughter. Unable to get her old car started Sarah and I helped to push it from where it was garaged in the old stable. In the Big House half a mile away down the hill their suitcases waited, ready for off. There was a level area of ground in front of the stable and Mrs Anstruther got out to help us get the car to the top of the hill. Unfortunately, she did not get back inside in time when the car started to go down the hill.

Off it set on its own, gathering speed, with the surly and belligerent Badger barking non-stop as he sat in state on the rear seat, weaving from side to side on the narrow driveway, all of a sudden running to the right to plunge down a steep bank. Crashing through a tangle of nettles, hazel bushes and blackberries the car came to an abrupt halt, its nose buried in a stinking marsh at the side of a deep ditch. Badger's muffled barking could still be heard as the mud plopped and spluttered and the car settled in its evil-smelling resting place. We looked at each other; and began to laugh.

It took a tractor from the Home Farm, yards of stout chain,

several men and a considerable number of bottles of beer before the little car was withdrawn from the dark-green slime, like some infant monster being dragged reluctantly from its malodorous lair. After the bodywork had been hosed down and the last traces of mud washed away the engine started at the first attempt; and three hours late Mrs Anstruther, still laughing and joking about what had happened, and Sarah departed.

Before they left Mrs Anstruther hugged me against her amply padded figure and stroked my hair. Sarah held me tight and kissed me on the lips. I had no wish to cry; but I did. The tears were there, rolling down my cheeks, and there was nothing I could do to prevent them falling.

I waved at the back of the little car as it disappeared among the trees and two handkerchiefs, held by outstretched arms, one on either side, fluttered in the breeze. The warm touch of her lips against mine faded quickly, but the memory of that kiss – the final kiss – and of the girl called Sarah who had meant so much to me was to stay intact within my mind for as long as I cared to remember. In one way, at least, I was never to forget the solemn pledge made between us on that first, hot summer's day when we lay on the grass beside a waterfall and love was something precious; both acute pleasure and deep, burning, aching pain.